My Vision, My Plan, MY NOW

Motivation You Need to Take the Action You Want

My Vision, My Plan, MY NOW

Motivation You Need to Take the Action You Want

Moovin4ward Publishing
Huntsville, Alabama

Copyright 2012 Moovin4ward Publishing

Library of Congress Control Number: 2012922450

ISBN: Paperback   978-0-9884564-19
       eBook   987-0-9884564-57

Printed in the United States of America

All rights reserved. No part of this publication may be reproduced, stored in a retrieval system or transmitted in any form or by any means, electronic, mechanical, photocopying, recording or otherwise, without the written permission of the publisher.

Publisher:
    Moovin4ward Publishing
    A Division of Moovin4ward Presentations LLC
    www.Moovin4ward.com

Contents

Part 1: My Vision 7

   Insight Before Vision 9
   Destiny and Purpose..21
   Is Fear Bullying You? 33
   I AM! 39
   The Now Before the Vision..49
   FOCUS 57

Part 2: My Plan 67

   Chances, Choices, Change..69
   The Unicycle: When the Ordinary Just Won't Do 79
   Do you have your P.H.D? 89
   RAW...101
   The Chronicles of "X" 109
   Frustrated 121

Part 3: MY NOW 133

   What NOW? Using Life's Pitfalls to Fall Forward 135
   Redefining an Image...147
   Omnipresence... Now 155
   T.A.G. You're It!..167
   Wealth is a Journey 173
   Building a Winning Personal Brand in a Digital World.................183
   Is There a Book in You? 195

Part 1: My Vision

My Vision, My Plan, MY NOW

Insight Before Vision

Pamela Glowski

"Everything happens for a reason… there are no accidents."

In the course of our lifetime we encounter many persons who have a tremendous impact on our lives. I have been fortunate to have had many mentors, coaches, teachers, parents, and friends that have touched me, inspired me motivated me, and who have loved me, none of them as much as my friend Sam.

I have known Sam for as long as I remember, nearly all 45 years of my life. I don't remember a time when I felt like she wasn't a part of my life. I don't remember our first meeting and my first recollection of spending time with her was when we played with baby dolls in my room at about age 3.

I loved playing with Sam because she had an extraordinary imagination. She could take the most ordinary toys or the dreariest days and make them into sun-filled adventures. Sam was born with the ability to do that. I believe we are each born with certain "birthday gifts". These gifts are pre-programmed skills, talents, abilities and behavioral traits that no one else seems to have. Sam was not only born creative; she was curious, musically inclined, outgoing, and full of energy.

Sam was the kind of child adults liked to be around. She had learned through her strict upbringing that obedience brought her love and dessert! We were raised in the late 60's and early 70's when children were still supposed to be, "seen and not heard." It was the time of knowing that if you were a "good girl" and cleaned your plate, there was a reward! And Sam loved dessert!

I, on the other hand, always sort of resisted this theory. In fact, it always seemed to me that as we were growing up we were in constant conflict because we were told, "Do as I say", at the same time we were seeing around us in media and advertising that we were supposed to be, "free to be…" It was the dawn of the era when women's rights, equality among races, and free thinking were emerging.

Sometimes this was confusing. Sometimes it was liberating, exciting, and led us to a bit of rebellion. Sam was the good one. She played by the rules. She emulated her parents in most ways in staying true to the values her family held so dear. She attended church every Sunday, she did her best in school, she felt fulfilled when she donated her time to charity (even at a very young age), she baked cookies with her Grandma every holiday, and she was kind and thoughtful to me and all of our mutual friends.

I think, for all of us, doing "good" is inborn. We all want to do what is "right" and win the approval of those who matter to us. It seemed, in our time, doing good for others was the focus even if it meant that we didn't do what "felt good" for ourselves.

In school, at home, and in society we were told to put what others wanted us to do first, and obey. Sam did fine with this until about 8th grade. Her parents had convinced her that her path in life was to finish high school, find a suitable husband, have babies, and become someone's secretary.

My companion's family was a "steel family" and had made a tight, but comfortable living working hard. They lived in a small, suburban ranch style home and when her mother was 32 and learned to drive, they purchased their second car. They believed that by having a job, they were fortunate. There was no trust fund waiting for them, for college, so if they wanted anything in this world it was going to take a lot of time, sacrifice, and work.

Sam's mother was one of 9 children, her father one of four, and they were post-war children who had lived their childhoods on very minimal necessities, and virtually no luxuries. Everything that they had, they had worked for and they believed there was honor and pride in what they had accomplished. They had done better than their parents had and felt that they were well off.

Sam's parents were married at a young age and believed that once you had reached 18 that was just part of the plan.

In our neighborhood, once we were in elementary school, we started making friends who we found had very different family backgrounds than our blue collar families. Two of the families on our street were both "husband-wife" doctor teams. That was weird. Women who were doctors! We had friends whose dads were engineers.

Their dads went to work in suits and ties every day and their wives stayed at home taking care of the children and the home.

I gravitated toward the professional type of lifestyle. Well, the one like Mr. and Mrs. Jordan. Mr. Jordan would leave for work at about 8am and was home by about 6p, each day. He only worked Monday through Friday. Mrs. Jordan would make breakfast for the family, do the dishes, plant flowers in the yard, and always had long painted finger nails. She always smiled and seemed to be so happy and calm, though she was always cleaning, fixing, or doing something around the house.

Sam thought she was comfortable with her parents plan until we had the first meeting with our guidance counselors as we were preparing to enter high school.

I'll never forget when Sam came out of her meeting with Mrs. Jones. She looked absolutely shell shocked. Though we had seen at this point how other people lived, we never thought that any of those things were possibilities were for us. Now, remember, I mentioned earlier that Sam was creative! After all of the information about colleges, aptitude tests, and careers were shared with her, she said to me, "Did you know that there are people, including women, who think up and produce the commercials we see on TV?" I felt a little embarrassed that I didn't know this, but before I could respond she blurted out, "I WANT TO DO THAT! I will have to go to college and earn a degree, but I know I can do that!"

I was wondering if she had lost her mind, because all she had talked about was the fact that she was going to graduate high school, get married, have kids, and be a secretary, but she seemed so ALIVE!

My Vision, My Plan, MY NOW

It was as if a whole new world had opened up to her. It all seemed to make sense as I thought about it, too. She had always loved to draw, color, sing, make signs in the store we worked in, and I could see how it just seemed that it could be a natural thing for her.

The joy was short lived for Sam. She was so excited to share what she had learned and the possibilities for her future with her parents; she never anticipated the wall she would hit when she made her announcement.

Sam had to wait until the weekend to share her new "dream" with her mom and dad. Her mother worked nights for a local utility company and she wanted to share her goal with both of her parents at the same time. She had also needed to do some research to find out what she would have to do to go to college; where she would go to college. My friend had some pamphlets from the guidance team, but she had never known anyone who had gone to college before besides her teachers, the doctors and engineers on our street. She didn't feel comfortable talking to any of the neighbors, so she stuck with Mrs. Jones.

Mrs. Jones had given Sam as much information that she had on Ohio State University and their Marketing Degree Program. Sam was just amazed. OSU was so far from home; so different than home. She would have to live there. Was that appropriate for a young woman to do without being married? Sam had read about co-eds in some of the teen romance novels she had read and magazines she saw in the store. The thought of this type of "fantasy" lifestyle was just never introduced to her before.

13:

My Vision, My Plan, MY NOW

Once Sam had gathered all of her facts, she had let her parents know that she wanted to talk to them about her future and they all sat down in the kitchen. I still remember that kitchen because it was avocado green with gold linoleum. It was so 1970's, and the place that all family discussions took place.

As Sam started to tell her parents, on that January night, about the Marketing Career possibilities, potential for earning a living on her own, and what Mrs. Jones had shared with her about college, Sam's parents put a sharp and sudden end to the conversation. Sam's mom started shaking her head and said, "Sam, that's silly! We don't have any money to pay for you to go to college. You will have to go to work after high school and do what dad and I did. There is nothing more to discuss".

Sam walked away from the table because she knew better than to argue, and went into her room and behind closed doors, cried on her bed with her pamphlets in her hand.

The next morning Sam woke up to a bright sunny morning and the usual Sunday morning ritual of bacon and eggs, toast and 10am mass. As Sam was brushing her hair, she thought, "What was I thinking?" and put the pamphlets into the garbage can. We didn't discuss Ohio State anymore until our junior year.

We were now edging into the mid-80's. Sam had been enjoying high school. She was in band, was working, was getting decent grades, and had a very full social calendar. Sam was having fun and at the moment, there seemed no need to look any further than the day in front of her. That was until Mrs. Jones, the guidance counselor called her down to the office to discuss our senior year schedule.

14:

Sam had made it very clear to Mrs. Jones that she was not going to be able to go to college. Sam let her know that her parents didn't have the money to send her to college. She even said that she didn't want to go anymore. She asked Mrs. Jones to schedule her into the Clerical Vocational Program because she was going to be a secretary.

Sam didn't get the best grades, but when she worked hard she did pretty well. Mrs. Jones told her it was a waste of talent for her to be a secretary. Mrs. Jones almost became indignant suggesting that women were making a difference in business and in the world like never before. Women were working for companies in roles only men used to have. They were also having families along with their careers. It was the first time she had heard that she could "bring home the bacon…and fry it up in a pan".

After this discussion with Mrs. Jones, Sam started thinking of things she had never thought of before. In the past, she didn't really think too much about making a difference in the world. That was for people much bigger than she was. She was just one high school cheerleader, certainly not someone who was of any significance.

Confidence was never really Sam's strong suit. As I mentioned, she was an" OK" student. She wasn't blessed with a figure to die for and when it came to looks, let's just say she was rather plain. She was one of those people who had a smile and a sweet personality that made her prettier as you got to know her. Sam had a tendency to be somewhat moody and believed that everyone around her was a better person than she was.

At the age of 16, she was just focused on making others around her happy. If she focused on others, then it took her mind away from all of her flaws. As long as everyone around her was happy, then she felt good. Her motivations to this point were simply making enough money in her part-time job at a local ice cream store to be able to buy clothes, and spending time with her dog, friends, and family.

But there was something, a little voice in her head, that she squelched often, that told her that she was capable of more. The idea of being a secretary just didn't resonate with her anymore. In one of her lone acts of bravery, she decided to schedule herself into the College Prep courses instead of the Clerical Vocational Program. Sam didn't tell her parents and honestly they didn't push her too hard or pay attention to her studies. They believed she had to be just average to get a job in a secretarial pool.

At the end of her junior year, Sam started dating a boy who she had been friends with for years. His name was John and he made her feel very special when he was around. As they started getting more serious, he encouraged her to do well in school, and to find a way to go to college. Sam did well because she wanted to be as special as John believed she was. She also felt that John was probably the best guy she would ever meet.

John had an amazing family and they welcomed her into their hearts and their homes almost from day one. John's family was Italian and his mom taught her to cook things she hadn't ever had before. She told her that she was smart and that she had a "caring" heart.

By the end of the first semester in our senior year, Sam realized that she wanted family to be the center of her world. She was motivated by caring and doing things for the people that were close to her. She had realized that the pattern of "family" kept re-occurring. She and John were closer than ever and she believed that the part of the plan her parents wanted for her in regards to getting married and having kids was just a bit of time away.

By the beginning of 1985 she realized that most of her friends and young women she was meeting were all in some kind of career. After realizing that her parents were not going to be able to help her financially she decided that she would take some kind of action in order to go to college. She worked as much as she could and saved as much money as was possible.

Sam spoke to Mrs. Jones again and found that there were local schools that she could afford while she worked. Because of her deep desire to care for those around her, Sam decided that she could parlay that into a nursing career. Nursing would also enable her to have a family and work around them, like her mother had done. Sam applied for one local Jr. College and was accepted into their Nursing Program.

It seemed like this is what God and the rest of the world had wanted for her and she chose to accept this path. It was probably going to be way easier than 4 years of college, anyway. Sam had thought that by healing the sick, she would make a difference in the world. She would be spending her time unselfishly in service to others. She still loved the idea of being able to have a career in Marketing, but sometimes growing up meant choosing what is logical rather than what is a pipedream…right?

Shortly after graduating with an Associate's Degree in Nursing, Sam married John. They both worked very hard and had two children. They experienced some normal challenges in their marriage...Sam lost her mother when she was 30; they moved to a new neighborhood when their second child was born, they had car troubles on occasion, normal average stuff. Everything was "NORMAL" until John came home one day and found Sam in the kitchen crying at the table.

Sam was 34 years old at this point and had arrived home from an average day at work, about two hours before. The kids were playing at the neighbor's house. Dinner was ready, the table was set. Everything was just as usual and that was the problem.

Sam looked at John and as she wiped the tears from her eyes, she said, "I'm not happy".

Sam had realized that although she had the family she always wanted, she was not fulfilled in her professional life. She had grown resentful and angry with patients. She saw true accidents that were acts of God, but in most cases, people were in poor health because of their own choices. She couldn't understand why they didn't get that.

On this day, in the middle of checking a patient's chart, she realized the same thing about herself. Everything in her life was the way it was because of all of the choices and the chances she had made; she had allowed others to make for her all created her NOW.

She had heard from so many patients as they had tried to console themselves about the medical state of their loved ones that, "Everything happens for a reason. There are no accidents and she realized, that applies to all of life. We create our life with each choice, each decision we make, goal we achieve or don't pursue. Every day we are making decisions that shape our future. Where we are, is no accident.

I'm glad to tell you that Sam ended up going back to school. She is now a Marketing Executive for a major company. She and John are still happily married and their children are now in college, too.

I recently had the chance to have dinner with Sam and I asked her if she had to do it over again, what she would do differently. Here is what she said...

If I had to do it over again, I would have been BRAVER. Many of the decisions I made were made out of fear. I was afraid I would hurt someone I loved, lose something I loved, find out I was wrong in my choice, or fail.

I would have BELIEVED in the little voice that I was trying so often to squelch. It was trying to lead me down the right path, for me, the whole time.

I will never play the victim again. If I really want to do something, I will do it, no matter what I, or anyone thinks, says or believes...sometimes the worst enemy is oneself.

I would have been more persistent.

I wouldn't have compromised or settled.

I would have taken the time to know myself better, know my own feelings, to consider all options, so that I could have created a better plan to achieve my REAL goals.

I would make sure that I have the right insights into who I am before I set a plan.

Pamela Glowski

Pamela Glowski is currently an Executive in a Northeast Ohio Staffing Service, a Life and Business Coach, Entrepreneur, Wife and Mother.

Pamela's expertise is in Sales and Marketing though she originally had a career in healthcare. Pamela started her own business in the travel industry in 2005. She was featured for her direct sales success in and Home Business Connection Magazine in April of 2006 and in Simply Home in their "Leading Ladies" Series in 2007. Pamela has developed proven strategies and has been a trainer and featured speaker in several Direct Sales Events including webinars, conference calls and live appearances. Pamela has created tele-workshops, group coaching sessions and offers One-on-One Coaching through her Life Coaching company Serene Insights. Pamela has used her training and coaching techniques to develop and grow her employers corporate sales team, many successful entrepreneurs, and looks forward to assisting you in "Creating the Life YOU Can't Wait to live!"

pamelaglowski@gmail.com

My Vision, My Plan, MY NOW

Destiny and Purpose

Frank Simmons

I believe that it is necessary for us to define <u>*Destiny*</u>. Destiny is defined as that place to which any person is destined. That sounds simple enough, but let's look deeper. To be destined means to be bound for an appointed place or assigned to go to a place designated. I believe that each one of us has been assigned to go to a designated place. We have been uniquely gifted and talented to get to that place. The place to which I am designated to go is not the same as yours. Therefore, it becomes crucial that you define YOUR destiny. Do you have a destiny plan?

To define something means to determine or identify the essential qualities of; to fix or mark the limits of; to make distinct, clear, or detailed. So, what does that mean? It means that we must clearly and distinctly identify the essential qualities of our destiny and fix or mark the limits (if there are any). Here are 5 questions to help you define YOUR destiny and come up with a destiny plan:

1. If you had the opportunity to do anything you wanted to do in your life, what would it be and why?
2. What have been the most satisfying moments or experiences in your life (business and/or personal)?

3. What types of people are you most comfortable with?
4. In what types of situations do you feel most comfortable (business and/or personal)?
5. What is your passion?

I think that we spend more time planning our next summer vacation than we do in planning our destination in life. When we get asked where we are going with our life, our life does not always get the same exciting response as our vacation. Get excited about the life that you are supposed to be living. The way you do that is to know where you are going. We look up directions for any place we want to go. There are some of you that get 2 or 3 different routes to get there – just in case. But, when it comes to our life – our destiny, many of us don't even have 1 complete set of directions.

No plan equals a lot of panic, sweat, and frustration. Where... Are... You... Going? Do you know the answer to that question? We spend a great part of our lives trying to figure that out and by the time a lot of us do figure it out we feel too tired to pursue it and give up. That is the wrong thing to do! Don't drift off to sleep and end up driving the wrong way until you run out of gas. WAKE UP! No matter where you are in life you can still get in hot pursuit of your destiny. It is never too late and you are never too far off track that you can't get back on.

Let the light come on for you and pursue YOUR destiny with all you have in you. *Your destiny is waiting on you to arrive.*

Ability

Ability is defined as the quality or state of being able physically and mentally. It is a competence, natural aptitude, or acquired proficiency. Ability is both a good thing and a bad thing at the same time. On one hand it is great to have ability and on the other hand ability can be a hindrance to you reaching your destiny. The ability to do more than one thing well can often cloud your vision of the destiny that awaits you. After a while do you know what this will do to a person? It forces them to be a jack of all and a master of none - thereby, throwing a wrench in their destiny by inducing confusion. I had ability, motivation, and attitude but, I still was not getting where I was supposed to because I had not _focused_ my abilities on a particular destiny.

Focus is defined as a concentrated effort or attention on a particular thing. It means to adjust your vision so that you can see clearly and sharply. Lack of focus can be one of the biggest obstacles on the path to our destiny. For many of us trying to focus on anything is very difficult given all of the things that go on in our lives. At any given moment we can become overwhelmed by...life. ? Are there so many things going on that your vision is blurred and you can't concentrate your efforts on a particular thing?

The absence of focus results in frustration, anger, and disappointment. Believe me, I know! But, the ability to focus results in reached goals and reached destiny. It results in a healthier and happier life. Think about and then let's do it. FOCUS!

Assessment

To assess your abilities is to have a critical appraisal for the purpose of understanding or interpreting. It is a guide for taking action. I believe that we all are uniquely gifted and talented for the destiny that waits us. What I want you to do now is take a long honest look at yourself and your abilities for the purpose of understanding and taking action.

The following five questions will help you to get a better understanding of some areas in which you are gifted or not and whether or not you do what you do based on what is right for you or what other people think is right for you.

Abilities

1. List all of the things that _you_ like to do.
2. List all of the things that _people say_ you are good at.
3. List all of the things you _are_ good at.
4. What are the things that come naturally to you?
5. List all of the things that you are interested in doing but, have never really tried to do for some reason?

What I am trying to do is get you to find out everything that you need to know about yourself so that you can get to your designated place.

Fear

What is fear? It is defined as an unpleasant emotion or thought that you have when you are frightened or worried by something dangerous, painful or bad that is happening or **might** happen. Pay close attention to the word **might**. Might means the possibility that something will happen or be done, or that something is true *although not very likely*. NOT VERY LIKELY! We are having unpleasant emotions and thoughts about things that are not likely to happen.

I believe that fear is that thing that grips your heart (the place where dreams and visions originate) and attacks it. It is that thing that tells you or convinces you that you cannot, should not, and will not be able to accomplish or achieve anything. It is that thing that tells you to give up, quit, and throw in the towel. Fear can stop you from achieving your goals and stop you from dreaming. If it does allow you to dream then, it causes those dreams to become nightmares.

What Are You Afraid Of?

What are you so afraid of that you are not pursuing your purpose in life? What is/are the thing/things that will not let you move forward into your destiny? I want you to take a moment and list the things that cause you fear. List everything you can think of from ants to zebras (that's A –Z). Next to the fear, I want you to write down the reason why. Don't be so shallow, surface, or superficial. List everything! Now, go back and prioritize that list from most fear to least fear.

If we don't get a grip on the fear that torments us it will get a grip on us. Fear is a nasty competitor. It plays a dirty game. Fear wants to take your dreams and visions captive so that you will not arrive at your assigned destination. It can sap the life out of you one drop at a time until there is no desire left in you to accomplish your goals, achieve your dreams, or go after your destiny.

Here is a 4 step process to follow to deal with your fear:

1. Identify it
2. Visualize it
3. Face it
4. Destroy it

The Past

The past is defined as a time gone by; a time that no longer exists; no longer current. The past is a place where some people continue to live which causes them to never enter into the fruitfulness of the present or future. It is a place where some never want to leave and a place that some want to forget everything about and never return again. I believe that it is necessary for us to go to the past to part with the past. I don't believe that it is something that must be ignored all together. It is necessary to have a balance in all things. This includes our dealing with the past. Dealing with the past means that we must take into account all of the things – ups, downs, ins, and outs that have impacted our lives.

The past is a strange place. In it there are good things and bad things. I don't believe that there is anyone who can honestly say that the past has not affected them at all. Our experiences, successes, and failures of the past have helped to shape who we are today. The things that we experience today will have an impact on who we are in the future. In the end, it is not the things that happen to us but, how we respond to the things that happen to us. We must, therefore, learn how to have a right assessment and perspective of the past events of our lives.

One of the major problems with the past is that we were once someone that many people refuse to forget. This is one of the major strongholds of the past – other people's memories of who you were. They will try to keep you there and if you are not careful you will become a hostage of other people's memories. Don't let that happen to you. We are only looking back to get a perspective of who you were and what has shaped you into who you are.

The reality is that many people are stuck. Whether you are stuck on your success or on your failure – you are stuck. The beauty of life is that we grow and change. We evolve and experience new and exciting things. If you can't, then you are stuck. It is sad. But, it is not the end. You can become unstuck.

To effectively get unstuck, we must first do some mind and heart cleansing. Our minds and hearts, where the past resides, must be reconditioned. We must take the things that happened and look at them with the right perspective. The events of your life were not meant to destroy you. They were meant to make you stronger. As you look back over your life and begin the process of parting with your past, you must be able to realize that the experiences that you went through all had purpose. This is probably the most difficult step in making it to your destiny. But, if you can make a separation and distinction between what was, is, and will be I believe you will make it to your destiny. Look at your past with a different perspective and determine how it is going to help you get to your final destination. If you can, the past can become a tool to carry you into the destiny that awaits you.

The Now

John Maxwell Has a book entitled "Today Matters". Do you believe that today is the most important day – that NOW is the most important time? Now is defined as this present moment. The moment that we live in, in my opinion, is the most crucial time in our lives.

Now is filled with enough things to keep us occupied for the rest of our lives. Now leads to the future and turns into the past very quickly. Therefore, if we don't make the most of our now - our yesterdays will become bad memories, which will try to attach themselves to our heart and mind, and our tomorrows will become nightmares.

The strange thing about now is that it is always now. Now never goes away. It is there staring us in the face and begging us to do something worthwhile with it. So, what are you going to do with the now moments of your life? How are you going to navigate now?

The Future

The future, simply put, means a time yet to come. It comes about as a result of the things that were done in our Past and are being done in the Now. A lot of people believe that the future is some undetermined place that can never be known. Do you believe that? If that is true, then, we are all doomed to never reach our destination. I believe that the future is a place that, if planned for, projected, and expected, can always be known. I personally do not like to be in the dark especially when it comes to my life. I would rather have the satisfaction of knowing that the future is something that did not creep up on me and catch me by surprise. But, caught by surprise is what many people think happens to them. NOT TRUE. They were not caught by surprise at all.

They should have seen it (the future) coming from a mile away. The future is not some distant unknown place where people just end up. It is a place that is created.

Once you have cleared the fog of things that keep you from focusing on you future, there are 3 things that you can do to for your future – Plan it, Project it, and Expect it.

Plan It

Plans have to be made in advance if the building project is going to be successful. The same is true for your future. If your future is going to be successful it must be planned.

Project It

To project something means to display it outwardly especially to an audience. This is where a lot of people miss the mark. As long as something is unknown to everybody else (a secret) then we are not responsible for it. As long as you don't tell anyone of your plans, if they don't happen, no one will ever know. It takes courage to broadcast you plan – to project it. If you want to see the future come into existence then you must project it.

Expect It

If you have done the work ahead of time in planning and projecting then, you can expect with a high degree of certainty that the thing you said would happen – will happen. It will happen because you have visualized it and prepared for it. To focus on your future means that you are putting together a plan today to ensure that your tomorrow will be better.

Never Give Up

Every person reading this must understand that there are obstacles on the road to your destiny. I am going to give you a minute or so to list some possible obstacles that might be on your particular road to your destiny. Three of the biggest obstacles you will face will be family, friends, and finances.

But wait, there is one more obstacle. So, make it four things I want to share with you that are obstacles. YOU. You, sometimes, are the biggest obstacle on the path to your destiny. You get in the way too much. You have too much to say. You do too much. You think too much. You analyze too much. You panic too much.

Now that you know some of the potential obstacles, let's obliterate them. That simply means to eliminate them, destroy them, or reduce them to nothing. Are you saying that I have to destroy my family? Absolutely not. I am saying that you must reduce the influence that the family has over your life. You have to reduce the influence of past friends in your life that want to keep you as bullet head, t-bone, or tank. The influence is too great and it makes it difficult for you to reach your destiny. The finance illusion must be dismantled. You have to talk back to this obstacle because it is talking to you. When faced with the illusion of lack of finance – move forward. Remember finance follows destiny.

Frank, all of that sounds good but, how do I deal with me? You have to reduce you own influence over your destiny. Wait a minute, Frank. It is my destiny. How do I reduce my influence over something that belongs to me? The way you do that is to quit analyzing, dissecting, and destroying everything that you don't understand. There are going to be some things that you do not understand along the way. It is up to you to navigate and pursue – not stall out in indecision. Get a grip on your mind and don't let it allow you to miss your destiny. If you can conquer the obstacle within, you will be able to get somewhere.

Some of us just give up to easily. The fact is that the struggle makes us stronger for the course. You have cried for help so many times and skipped so many processes that you are about to die. You're not dying because what you are going through right now is tough. You are dying because you yelled uncle and someone came and cut you out of the cocoon and your wings aren't strong enough to fly. Embrace the struggle because it will make you stronger.

There are three things that are going to help you not give up - patience, partnership, and persistence. Patience will help you line up your thoughts and keep you from making rash mistakes and decisions. Partnership will give you someone to hold you accountable, someone to challenge you, and someone to encourage you. Persistence is more attitude than action and this attitude will keep you from giving up.

You CAN reach your destiny!

FRANK SIMMONS

Frank Simmons, Jr. is a speaker, trainer, coach, mentor, author, and motivator. He has been married to his wife, Angela for 28 years. Frank has traveled extensively throughout the United States speaking to audiences of all ages and backgrounds.

He worked for Monster Worldwide as a Speaker, Trainer, and Area Manager providing national speaker training and coaching and speaking to high school and college students, parents and staff as well as speaking for organizations such as Bank of America, the Equal Employment Opportunity Council and others.

Frank is the Chief Inspirational Officer for Frankly Speaking Seminars where he works with his wife to provide workshops, seminars, coaching, training, and keynotes. He and his wife are also singers and songwriters with 2 CD's. Frank is the author and co-author of 3 books - *The Man of Destiny*, *Unleash the Greatness Within You*, and *Pursue IT with All You've Got*.

    www.franklyspeakingseminars.com
    www.facebook.com/frankspeaks
    frank_speaks@yahoo.com

Is Fear Bullying You?
Elisa Gary

To starve one thing, is to feed another. This saying is true in every aspect of our lives; whether its in context of your career, relationships, academics, or the interpersonal struggles associated with religion and morality. One thing remains constant among each of these, that is the unavoidable occupation of choice. This very word freezes many dead in their tracks. The ability to distinguish between wants and needs, caring for others and the fulfillment of self-gratification is daunting at best. Adding the stress of committing to one reality over another brings on a far more difficult task, conquering fear. When you make a decision, you feed the opportunities of that decision and ultimately reap the rewards associated with it. In contrast the paths you reject, aborts the possible outcomes of those choices, both good and bad. Although alternate decisions can yield similar outcomes, surely there will be different experiences associated with each chosen path.

Taking the time to determine your wants, and mapping out a course of action towards attaining your goal will propel you towards your dreams. Although fear can take many forms, it most commonly presents as a side effect of one or more pre-existing conditions. These include rejection, doing it alone, failure, the perception of others, being too late and lastly success. Any one or combination of these can induce a fear frenzy and stall progress towards attaining your goals.

Fear of Rejection

Most people like to believe that they are relatively liked within their immediate communities. For some, professional community takes precedence over personal or academic, and others vice versa. Despite these preferences, acceptance does affect our gages of goal achievement. Though acceptance does present a powerful dynamic when it comes to decision making, it should not be the sole determining factor in your aborting a viable choice, and subsequent path toward your goals. Rejection is a reality. This is a truth that each of us must come to terms with. For everyone that will tell you yes, there will be ten people that will scream no. To overcome this fear, constantly remind yourself that there is a reward for the persistent. Perhaps the path, which you so desperately sought to take in attaining your goal, did not work out. Continue to pursue your dream, don't give up and remember to never reject yourself.

Fear of Doing it Alone

We have all heard the saying "Two heads are better than one", but sometimes the road to success is a cold and lonely one. Having someone to bounce ideas off of is great. Building a support system is an excellent way to keep you motivated, grounded and focused. However, it is reasonable to assume that most of the hard work associated with your dream will need to be done by you. Quite frankly, few may prove to be genuinely interested in your aspirations. This is the time to do a serious gut check. Remind yourself why you are so passionate about your goal.

What are you seeking to gain by achieving it? Sometimes the only way to get started is to do so alone. Keeping that in mind, being a jack of all trades is not the best way to navigate your way to success.

Focus on what you do best, and utilize your resources to find the people and assets needed to get the job done. Although it is tempting to be "hands on" with every aspect of your dream, this can diminish the immensely hard work you have devoted thus far.

Fear of Failure

Someone once told me, "A sure sign that something is worth going after, is when you have every reason to believe you will fail". What I have learned since then, is that failure is simply an unsuccessful attempt at a course of action toward your goal. It is not uncommon to speak to others who have overcome adversity, and faced extenuating circumstances; which they presumed would all but pulverize the chances they had at succeeding. It is these same people who will attest that the very thing that seemed to be their demise, revamped their thinking, fueled their hunger to overcome these adversities, and embarked them on a new path which ended in goal fulfillment. Failure is like trash. It's dirty and messy, but if you go through the rubble, there is plenty to recycle and start again.

Fear of the Perception of Others

When I was younger, I had an extremely high affinity for pleasing others. No matter what I was involved in, I always wanted to be amongst those who would acknowledge my good deeds, applaud my achievements, and reward my hard work. As I got older, and a tad bit wiser, I learned that this simply was a superficial and external means of motivating myself. The same applies to you and your dream. Whatever goal you have set for yourself is just that, your goal! Don't be consumed with the solicited praise of others. While public recognition of your accomplishments will increase your self-esteem, dependency on it will ruin your vision, and alter your course of action. Your work will no longer be driven by your determination to overcome adversity, beating the odds, and realizing your vision. Instead, it will be watered down with half baked work and bottomless praise.

Fear of Being to Late

In a world that has been flooded with technology, which for many resulted in job loss, there is a much greater desire to find alternate ways to support ourselves financially. You may be one of those people who are fed up with the traditional nine to five, but you think it's' just too late to pursue anything else. Remember failure is like trash, it can be recycled. If your current job gave you a pink slip, flip it over and start mapping your plan of action. Start that business you've been dreaming about, go back to school, apply for the position you were too afraid to leave your current job for. Whatever you do, don't trick yourself into believing that it's too late to do something about your situation. It is never too late to pursue a dream. Each day is an opportunity to forge an attack on your doubts and push full steam ahead toward your aspirations.

Fear of Success

So you've done it. You stuck it out, and now you've accomplished what you set out to do. The only problem is that your success has brought on quite a bit more responsibility, time commitment, study hours, work hours, training, monetary burden, et cetera than you expected.

For many, this is the time that it seems terribly convenient to make excuses and revert to your previous course of do nothing and procrastination. However, I implore you to push forward and utilize your support system. Don't become overwhelmed with your new reality. Take the time to regroup, plan, if need be reorganize your support team, and above all enjoy your accomplishment.

ELISA S. GARY

Elisa, Director of *"The 1st Ministry Initiative,"* is a woman with a passion for God, people and the restoration of families. She has branded herself as an Inspiration Coach, noting that "motivation is external, but inspiration comes from within". She hosts weekly conference calls, during which she delivers powerful lessons; challenging her  listeners to push past their current circumstance, make their mess their message, and to be actively engaged in their lives. In November 2011 Elisa founded *The 1st Ministry Initiative*. Her organization encourages self-development, overcoming obstacles, and mental well-being. Elisa firmly believes suffering in silence, voids your testimony and inhibits personal break-through. Her new book "What God Brings Together…" which focuses on marriage will be released in April 2013. Find out more by visiting **www.thecompletewomanfellowship.com**.

My Vision, My Plan, MY NOW

38:

My Vision, My Plan, MY NOW

I AM!

Dr. Kreslyn Kelley

I am hungry. I am sleepy. I am sad. I am bored. We all declare to be something at some point throughout the days of our lives. "I am" is one of the simplest affirmations we make to reinforce to ourselves what is going on in our minds and to inform others of the same. Most "I am" statements are made, however, about "how" we feel, what we see, and what we hear. Such statements pertain to our senses. Rarely, do we make assertions about "who" I am. When we do, they are often still reflective of how we feel. For instance, "I am human" is a "who I am" statement that is often used by someone after they've made an offense towards another. In another instance, "I am love" is typically stated to express the feeling of love, not the state of being. Yes, we are human, but we are also spiritual. We are love, because God is Love and we are made in his image. There is no right or wrong "I am" statement, but it is critically important to pay attention to the statements we make about ourselves if we would like to realize our grandest dreams. If we want to call into action our visions and craft plans that will make our ideas a reality, then we must verbally report truths about who we are, and they must be specific to that which we desire.

When acknowledging truths, one must be careful about what is taken into the mind through the eyes, ears, and hearts. In fact, to establish realistic "I am" statements for yourself, you may want to consider turning away from the images portrayed on the television, which depict false imagery and lavish life-styles of people who appear to have a good time, for a living, and do no work to earn that right. It is also past time to erase the negative comments made to you by your childhood friends and classmates, who, all throughout grade-school, repeated to you hundreds of times, "you're ugly", "you're dumb", "you're skinny", "you're fat". What about the comments made by parents and family patriarchs and matriarchs and were reiterated at every family gathering that you are just like your dad, your mom, your uncle, aunt, or grandfather. Whether you considered the "you are" statements negative or positive, admirable, or degrading, you probably bought into them whether you hated the comparisons or liked them, approved them or rejected them. And, unless, you learned to art of self-referral or self-talk very early in life, you still live with much of those endorsements today.

In the comedic, yet dramatic, movie and stage play, Madea's Family Reunion by Tyler Perry, Madea, the main character, finds her life unexpectedly shifted by the assignment of a court judge to take on the role of foster parent. The young girl she is to parent is a troubled teen, who hid her fear of what others thought of her with bouts of fury, sarcasm, fighting, and underachievement. The young lady had obviously heard many "you are" statements from family, classmates, and others, because in one scene, after she starts to experience a little success, she expressed these fears to Madea. Madea, then, gave her a little nudge of encouragement with what I consider to be a very profound statement, and one that I now often use. She simply told her, "Folk gon' talk about you til the day you die. Ain't nothing you can do about it. But, it ain't what people call you; it's what you answer to." You see, though it is flattering to be told you are just like someone else, whom you admire, unfortunately many have not been lavished with "you are" statements that are oh so gratifying, but have been demeaned and adversely compared early in life by friends, family member and strangers, and some for long periods of time. The fact of the matter is, whether negatively or positively associated, no one is an exact replica of anyone else, not even if an identical twin. No one else has ever or will ever have your finger print, so you are designed to be who you are. But, only you get to decide who that is.

Those persons, who have heard copious amounts of negativity, find it challenging and nearly impossible to create "I am" statements that defy the lies spoken to them. I was one of those individuals. While growing up, I was told that I was pretty, but too skinny. I was told that I was smart, but I didn't have anything. These were all true statements, I might add; and even when I tried to hold my head up in spite of the criticism, I was then told that I thought I was some prima donna, yet another dishonor to attempt to overcome. Consequently, I was underequipped and inexperienced in my emotional and spiritual capacity to rise above the fray and keep my heart and mind intact; and, the coping skills I developed cost me significantly throughout my young adult life as I often played small so that others could feel larger than life. Sometimes, coping would reflect itself as arrogance, sometimes uncontrollable anger, sometimes negative attention seeking behaviors. Ridicule and comparison really took their toll on me, and simply put, they took their toll on everyone in some fashion.

To add insult to injury, we typically do not negate the maltreatment, but we learn it. So, we not only buy into what we've been told by others, but we begin to judge and compare ourselves and others accordingly. It's almost impossible not to, because without effective intervention, hurt people hurt people. Furthermore, it is what we feed ourselves, daily, via our television, music, and print we read. There are consistent images of what society and others tell us is beautiful, smart, acceptable, and hip; and, unless, we practice affirming ourselves, daily, then we will never think that we are good enough.

In my personal struggle for significance I achieved many things in life. I've driven fine cars and lived in suburban homes while still feeling the brunt of not thinking I was up to par. I knew better in my heart, but it took years of positive self-talk before I actually believed. One of the books I discovered a couple years ago, which helped me tremendously with this is, *The Master Key System*, by Charles Hannel. He shared an affirmation practiced by a young man, who at the age of 13, was told by many doctors, he was ill and cripple, and there was no possibility he'd get better. The seemingly hopeless child, chose to refute the medical report by using sustaining words which were opposite of the information being articulated to him and his mother. He began to encourage himself with the qualities he needed to beat the odds. His words were simple: "I am whole, perfect, strong, powerful, loving, happy, and harmonious." He affirmed himself over and over again, while going to sleep, upon awaking, and all throughout the day, but he didn't stop there. Just like people generally criticize others the way they criticize themselves, he encouraged others the same as he did himself. Long story short, he defied all that the doctors portended and was made whole in just a few years and grew to be a healthy adult. Healthy self-referral and self-talk is imperative to realizing our dreams, but also a strong indicator of how well we relate to others.

If the statement "you are" is powerful for those who believe what others say about them, then how much more powerful is the statement, "I am" for those who choose to believe with steadfast faith that they are who they say they are. When we speak, things happen! I owned these words for myself the very first time I read them, and now I repeat them daily. I am who I say I am. This does not mean that I speak negatively to others when they say I remind them of my mother, father, grandmother, or other family members or when people ridicule me or speak their wishes for my life. It is just that I take the attributes from their remarks that I choose to own and those that align with what I say about myself and then consciously dismiss the rest without rebuttal. Fortunately, truth says that I get to choose who I am. You get to choose who you are. Though it is a challenging task to rest in your claim of who that is, it is not an impossible one. In fact it is conceivable to realize any dream you choose by simply stating, with courage, determination, resilience, perseverance, and faith, "I am" followed by whatever you wish to be.

The education that I received was because I spoke my desires and intentions and then moved in faith. The material items I possess were first a desire, then a spoken work, and then actions followed to make them happen. Even, the hard things that I've endured, like sickness, divorce, and other broken relationships were first a forethought, a verbal expression, and then magical steps toward them were inevitable. The same is true for your own life, whether you admit it or not. As Mahatma Gandhi stated so eloquently, "Your beliefs become your thoughts, your thoughts become your words, your words become your actions, your actions become your habits, your habits become your values, your values become your destiny." So, for some us, to get what we want and be who we wish to be, need to do more than change what we think, we need to change what we believe. If you believe that you are supposed to be poor or that anybody is, for that matter, then you will have thoughts of poverty, speak words of poverty, habitually, act impoverished, and certainly be poor. If you wish to be wealthy, you must first change what you believe about poverty and wealth.

Overwhelming thoughts of lack, insecurity, underachievement, sorrow, discouragement, fear, and pain have been taught to many of us throughout our life time, so it is not abnormal to hold such things in your mind. We create some of these own ideals ourselves to protect us, after we've experienced pain and disappointment. Some of us have been subjected to so much of it that we even think that we are undeserving of anything good or of receiving anything we desire. Again, if this is what you believe, then this is what you will receive. They are truths if you believe them to be truth and lies if you believe them to be lies. You truly have the right to decide and your actions will be head on in accordance with that decision.

Since I choose to think abundance, joy, love, peace, and harmony, I've been asked by many, "how do you stay so positive all the time?" My response is, "I am not positive "all" the time, but I am most of the time, because I'd rather think positive thoughts and be happy and receive some of what I expect from that than to think negatively and be unhappy, sick, and disgusted most of the time. In my thinking, I set my hopes high. Who cares if I reach the moon or not? If I aim for it, at the very least, I will most certainly reach the space stratosphere. I decide who "I am", what I want, and I hold fast to that. My declaration has served me well, lifting me out of poverty, out of despair, out of depression, out of despondency, out of delusion. Yes, delusion! To think that you have no control over your destiny is delusional!!! It's a figment of your imagination. You've either been taught that or you imagined it yourself. So, it may be your reality, but it is also one big lie.

The truth is, and this is in both the scientific and spiritual senses, so follow it with whatever belief system you choose. No one else has your DNA, never have and never will. Therefore, you are uniquely designed to be someone that no one else can be. That makes you special! You possess a set of attributes, experiences, personality traits, and the combination of them all that no one else has. That's why it is puzzling to me when people single out another because of their differences. The fact is, we are all eccentric. When someone starts a business, a coach will ask them, "What makes your product different from your competitor's?" They will tell you that being different and having a competitive edge are vitally important for marketing your business and creating a product that will help you thrive as a business owner. So, why not embrace our own diversity? It makes you relevant. What makes us different is what makes us special, needed, and appreciated. What a boring world this would be if we all were just alike? What lack we would experience if we all had the same skill set, knowledge, and experiences? Accepting what makes us irreplaceable is attractive and makes us happy with being who we are, and that alone is sheer fortune. Without it, elaborate dreams may never be realized.

When understanding you are relevant, you also understand that you are of value. You have worth; therefore, you are worthy to receive in harmony with that which you give. Everyone has worth. I know you may disagree with that statement as someone may have come to mind when you read it; but, the most negative person that you may deem unworthy, first considered himself unworthy, then actions followed to support his "I am" statements or the "you are" statements that he never rejected. If you think you are unworthy, then someone else will believe the same about you. You're relevant and you're worthy, not because of your personality, your talents, your education nor because of your lineage. It's the "You" that makes you worthy. The unique you and your real state-of-being.

You are not only unique, but you are powerful. The very fact that you can think something into existence illustrates such power. Many of us have practiced misusing our authority by giving it to others by believing the ideals they have placed in our heads and believing the ideals we've placed in our own heads. At the end of the day, we are what we have created ourselves to be. However, if we would only know and believe who we really are, those ideals would not carry the amount of weight that they do. We were made in the image of God and empowered to do what he's done: Create. We are pure spirit, and have the power of life and death in the words we speak. Our being is much more divine than the heavens we create and far more influential than the hells we make for ourselves. But, one will never realize it until he proclaims that "I am..." I am worthy! I am relevant! I am powerful! I am made in God's image and can create whatever I want for my life! Learning to think, speak, and act as though we believe the aforementioned statements is the step needed to bring visions into reality, plans into action, and tomorrow into today.

I personally know this to be true, as I have recreated myself numerous times. Having a father that committed suicide after his second attempt, when I was only 11 years of age, and knowing that several family member struggled with mental illness, I could have opted to give up on life every time it became challenging for me, but I chose to hold on to faith. As a teenager, I toyed with the thought of suicide, but I also had positive thoughts of survival that I clung to instead. Now, at the age of 42 I have not had such thoughts since. I am an overcomer. I AM!

I fought against sickness and disease during my early teenage years and was told by doctors, when diagnosed with Chrohn's disease, that it was incurable and I may be on medication the rest of my life. Yet, today, I have not taken medication for that ailment in over 23 years. I declared as a teenager, I am healed! I AM!

Even when, at the tender age of 22, I was a single parent of two children with meager means, I insisted on staying away from living in impoverished communities because I dreamed of raising my children in safe communities with high achieving schools. I could have used the excuse that their father wasn't active in their life and that child support was there, but wasn't enough to really live the lifestyle that I wanted for them as a reason to take an easier route. But, I am responsible and must make this happen. I am in control. I AM!

As a child who lived in a very low middle class/high lower class, blended family, in a community where many friends did not graduate from high school, and some struggled with drug addictions, and even went to prison, I still managed to graduate from high school and earn three college degrees. I could have easily chosen to be a product of my environment, but I elected to think about things that could get me out of my environment. I declared that I am an achiever. I AM!

I have professed many job titles in several vocational fields, from an administrative clerk to graduate student, jewelry salesperson, make-up consultant, teacher, school principal, program director, and entrepreneur. However, lately, I have declared I am an empowerment coach, motivational speaker, activist, and author. And, because you are reading this chapter, know that my dreams are realized. My vision is now reality. My plan has unfolded. And, what I declared yesterday is happening today. It is my now. I AM!!

DR. KRESLYN KELLEY

Life experienced first, then, academically trained - Educator, Entrepreneur, Trainer, Mentor, Coach, Community Servant and Activist.

Kreslyn left the field of education, to start her own business, Premier Leadership Academy. Her passion is still educating children, but now also includes educating adults. Her platform has moved beyond the school house, to conference rooms, auditoriums, and office space. Her subject matter has changed from reading, writing and arithmetic to leadership, diversity, character building, team building, goal setting, and helping others identify individual purpose and passion. Dr. Kelley's ultimate goal, is always to help anyone seeking higher ground realize that it is not only possible, but it is inevitable! Her simple, yet dynamic, approach is making herself real and transparent to others by sharing her own stories of challenges and triumphs.

For more information, visit her site, **kreslynkelley.com**. or **placademy.net**.

The Now Before the Vision
Stephanie Logan

While I am all about having a vision and knowing where you may want to go in life; I think we all have to be aware of our now. Where we are now, how we deal with our now, and what we learn in the now will make our vision clearer. If we look at our failures and our successes we will be more equipped to reach our vision. But before we begin our NOW journey look at your vision: examine it closely and make sure that the vision you carry on this journey; it is yours and not someone else's vision. Many times in life we never make it to the vision because the vision we were trying to reach was not our own. So I ask you now to make sure and be clear that the vision you carry must be your own.

Now, that you have determined that the vision you carry is your own let's look at dealing with your now. Ask yourself are you doing what is needed to get to that vision now. Or is it your now that is blocking your vision. Your willingness to look at your darkness is what empowers you to change. The only way to get what you really want is to let go of what you don't want. Everything that happens to you is a reflection of what you believe about yourself. We cannot outperform our level of self-esteem. We cannot draw to ourselves more than we think we are worth. So be confident and know your worth.

On your journey to your vision you will encounter road blocks, obstacles, and setbacks; just know this is a part of the journey to the vision and no reason to turn around.

In life there are winners and losers and the sooner we realize that fact the better some of us will be.

My nine year-old gets rewarded at school for doing what he should already be doing anyway: listening, learning, and being respectful. He takes karate lessons and when they have tournaments all the kids that participate gets a trophy regardless of how they do. Does anyone see the problem with this "WE ALL ARE WINNERS" concept that is sweeping the nation? Am I the only person that thinks we should not reward people for the things they should be doing anyway? If everyone wins, why try harder than anyone else? What happens when you don't have the money to incentivize your kids to be good, go to school, listen to their teachers, or clean their room? I say we go back to the basics! Back to a time when we did right not because of promises of rewards or special perks, but simply because it is the right thing to do... a time when you earned a trophy, ribbon, or award because you were the best and not just because you showed up and participated. No worries. I have the perfect plan, mind set, and focus to get back to the basics. A way to determine who the real winner can and will be at the end of this process. Who knows, that winner just may be you.

Have a Plan

So where do you begin? Well I say start with a plan. Have a plan to figure out what you want to do and what it is you really want out of life, or, on a smaller scale, what you want right now. If this seems to be an impossible task, ask yourself this: What don't you want out of life? Let that be your starting point. Talk to people that did do or are doing what you want to do, and find out what they did or didn't do. Now, with that information you have the foundation for your plan. This may seem like an easy concept but think about all the times you were given advice by your parents, teachers, and many other adults, only to think (and in some cases say), "they don't know what they are talking about." We thought they were crazy. We felt like they did not, would not, and could not ever understand. Stop to think about this. Not much has changed where life experience is concerned. Those people wanted us to learn from their mistakes, their pain, and their heartache. They loved or cared enough about us not to want us to endure what they had already gone through.

This part of the plan is going to make you think I am off my rocker. It is this: the plan you have right now will change this very minute. It will not be the same plan at the end of your race. The road is the same but the journey will different for us all. Keep in mind change is all around us. Nothing lasts forever so embrace change and welcome it because it is change that moves us forward. Change makes us think outside of the box and with that thinking change will one day get us out of the box that life has put us in. Expect the unexpected so when change happens you will be ready to handle anything. Roll with the punches. If and when you hit a bump in the road, remember, it is not the end of the world. It is simply a lesson learned and one more step to building the perfect plan for you. Dare to dream! Develop your plan, write it down, and start now because today does matter. Today's plan will determine your tomorrow whether you know it or not.

Take Your Life Back

We all have missed opportunities in life not because of what we didn't know but because of what we were afraid to know. So to that I say, have no fear!

If you fail at something, learn from it and don't be afraid to try again. At least now you know what may or may not work. Think of failure as the tuition (price) you pay for success. If you never fail at anything how do you know when you improve or when you really have succeeded? If you never have any bad times then the good times won't seem so good. If it never rained then the sunny days would be just a regular unremarkable days. If no one ever died, birth would not be so special; plus the world would be super crowded! I could go on and on but the point I am making is we have to have contrast. You will lose some and win some. Our hope is to win more than we lose but if you are afraid to try and afraid to fail, you will never win.

Are you afraid to succeed because you are fearful of the unknown? Are you afraid of how success will change your life as you know it? How about being scared of how you will handle success? Being afraid of success makes me think of a poem by Jeremy Garnett, the founder of The Thomas Pivot Project:

Success

There is a sound that resounds in the back of my mind that echoes the voice of reason.

Through seasons, it develops, only to reflect the voice of one, who made the choice.

My Vision, My Plan, MY NOW

To dedicate more of life to the pseudo facade, than the actualities that are home to hidden realities.

What equips these illusions strengthens insecurity under vague scrutiny; this is tightly encased within me.

In the mirror, I see a noble reject who reflects an image brought on by a misguided quest.

Or, could this possibly be a quest-ion? Who is this; what is this?

I never thought, maybe that is the problem...I never thought! So in silence, it haunts -me; which brings this all back to me.

Each day, I live to fail and die to succeed. All along it was never the fear of failure that scares me, but success has always startled me.

I used to be concerned of what others thought of me. I was afraid of what they thought of what I was doing. I was worried they may laugh and think I was crazy. I was afraid they would not like me. Then one day I thought "Who the hell are THEY anyway? And why do I care what THEY think?" It was that day that changed my attitude; I started believing that THEY would either like me, support me, or not. If they chose not to then that was their loss not mine. You can no longer be afraid to take risks and chances. You can no longer be fearful of what others may say, think, or do. Remember this is your life and you control it. Being afraid gives others control of your life and your plans. So, I say today: TAKE YOUR LIFE BACK!!!

Be Your Biggest Fan

So you may be asking yourself, "How do I take my life back when I never knew I lost it?" When the world is against you or at least you think it is, remember you have to be your biggest fan. That way you always have someone in your corner. Then, when the chips are down and you think you have nowhere else to go, look inside yourself. If you don't trust and believe in yourself, who else will? If you don't invest in yourself, who else will? Be strong and steadfast in yourself, your dreams, and your plans. You must, at all times, have confidence that no matter what comes your way you will succeed and be the best. If for some chance that is not the outcome, slip on you cheerleading outfit, pick up your pom-poms and cheer yourself happy because you are now able to fight another day. To paraphrase Shakespeare: be true, be true to thine own self be true. Be more concerned with your character than your reputation because your character is who you really are, while your reputation is merely what others think of you! Just because you lose does not by any means make you a loser. If you fail, it does not make you a failure and the sooner you learn that lesson you can and will succeed in life in whatever you set your mind to do. One day you will know that the winner at the end of this process is none other than you! Relax. Get your game plan together, take your life back as you cheer yourself across the finish line, and be the winner you and I know you are.

"Place your faith in no man (or woman) and you will never know disappointment". I've taken this saying to heart when it comes to building my success. I no longer wait or depend on others to help me. If they do, that's great. If they don't, that's OK too since I wasn't banking on it anyway. For your success in your vision, place your faith in your own hands.

Depend on the one person that you know will never let you down...YOU! The greatest mental achievement is succeeding under your own power; knowing that it wasn't handed to you. When it is all said and done, rejoice in the fact that you don't owe anyone a thing.

Remember that words are powerful and the words you speak can help or hurt you. How do your words hurt you? As a matter of fact they can kill you. The negative words you speak can kill your spirits and dreams. So how can words help? The same concept of success is applied here. The positive words you speak can move you in the right direction by motivating and inspiring you to be all you can be, so when it is all said and done the winner will be at the end will be YOU!!! You be the person that speaks power, wisdom, and confidence to those around you. You can be the light that they are looking for and the light you need. Remember the race starts and ends with you. After all, it is your race to win or lose. I know you can do whatever you set your mind to do but the bigger and most important question is... Do you know *you* can do anything you set your mind to do? I hope you do because you have what it takes to succeed, be, do, and excel in whatever you want to in life. So please don't give that power - your power - away. Your vision is closer than you think...

Stephanie Logan

As an inspirational and motivational speaker, her unique presentation style is energetic, thought-provoking, challenging, content-rich and, at times, extremely humorous. Whether designed as a keynote speech, conference session, special church program, seminar, symposium or corporate retreat, each presentation is uniquely planned to encourage, educate, enlighten and empower the audience to action. Stephanie draws upon her diverse background to relate key principles, while enriching her content with insightful and dramatic illustrations, stories and humor.

Although Stephanie's presentations are always fascinating and an enjoyable experience, she believes that the true success of any speaking engagement can only be judged by its lasting effects. Speaking with over twenty years experience; Stephanie draws upon her own experiences to provide affective and effective content while equipping audiences with firsthand information.

FOCUS

Sharon A. Myers

Let's talk about success. Most people want it. Some people have even envisioned themselves in it. Yet, many people are just not willing to do what IT takes to make what they see in their heads a reality in their lives. Maybe it seems too far away. Maybe their view of it is blocked by obstructions. Or maybe they just need to FOCUS their view.

Beyond determining why you want it and how it fits in your overall purpose in life…

Beyond creating a plan with detailed SMART goals and an outline of the strategies you'll use to achieve your goals…

You need to see it. You need to FOCUS your vision on your success.

F	Be Fearless
O	Be Optimistic
C	Be Confident
U	Be Unwavering
S	Be Strategic

Be Fearless.

Whether it's a fear of failure, fear of success, or fear of change... fear is poisonous and will slowly stop you in your tracks and prevent you from completing your journey to success.

One thing is certain, if you don't try, you'll never fail. But if you never try, you'll never succeed. Bill Cosby once said, "In order to succeed, your desire for success should be greater than your fear of failure." You won't achieve success if you do nothing. If you wait too long to get started, you open the door for doubt and more fear. But when you actually muster up enough courage to start implementing your plan and taking action, your confidence will grow.

Fears are something we all have and are told to "get over." Unfortunately, getting over them is easier said than done.

So here are some tips to help you overcome your fears:

Examine your fears. Lay them out on the table to determine why these fears have so much power over you. Examining your fears starts with being honest with yourself. Trying to convince yourself that the fear doesn't exist won't make it go away.

Educate yourself on the fear. Learn more about the origin of the fear and why you are so afraid. It could very well be something that you've experienced in your past. Educate yourself on all of the facts that make you fearful.

Develop faith in something. To face fears, you got to believe in something. Whether its religion or God; believe in something. When you find faith, you find a healthy way of making yourself feel as if nothing can go wrong. When you feel that way, you can then start facing your fears. You'll have a sense of feeling that everything will be okay.

Face your fear. What is the worst that can happen? Write down everything than can go wrong. Then come up with an action that would mitigate your worst case scenario. The point is, even if you fail, you still succeed. You gain character as a person when you face a challenge or fear.

Change your outlook. Don't think about the past and what has happened. You're just going backwards and that's exactly why you can't get over it. Most people don't remember things that have happened in the past about you, so why should you fixate on it? Have a positive attitude. Have a NOW attitude. Don't dwell on regrets, or you'll always have fears. Move forward in order to gain courage to face them.

Running away from your fears don't make them go away, that just makes them bigger than ever. Obviously we're never going to be completely fearless in everything we do... but we can at least make an effort to be more fearless.

Be Optimistic.

I always like to look on the optimistic side of life, but I am realistic enough to know that life is a complex matter. –Walt Disney

I'm probably the most pessimistic Optimist I know. I always expect the best outcome, but I plan for the worst outcome. I like to call it risk management, which makes it sound like it's okay. But having a tendency to always calculate risks, i.e. be pessimistic, can have major negative consequences on your life.

The Law of Attraction states that whatever you focus on and give your attention to, you attract more of into your life. So if you are always expecting the worst, you get the worst.

Meanwhile, someone who is optimistic is someone disposed to take a favorable view of events or conditions and to expect the most favorable outcome. This person is more likely to accept obstacles as challenges, and failures as lessons learned.

A great way to maintain an optimistic viewpoint is to practice visualizing your success. Take time to live in the moment of your success and engage in how you'll feel when you achieve it. For example, if your goal is to earn a Master's degree, imagine your graduation day. Imagine your loved ones cheering when your name is announced. Imagine walking across the stage and shaking the hand of the school's President. Imagine the pictures you'll take with your friends and family immediately after the ceremony. When you spend a few moments visualizing your success, you can not only see it, but also feel, touch, smell, and hear it.

Another great way to maintain optimism is to use positive affirmations. Affirmations are short positive statements that remind you of what you're trying to accomplish. Whether you purchase an affirmation book or read Proverbs in your Bible, daily affirmations have proven to keep you optimistic about life.

The best affirmations are the ones that you write yourself.

Here are a few tips to writing your own affirmations. Make sure the affirmation is:

About you. That may sound selfish, but your affirmation is to inspire YOU! It should not be about someone else or what someone else wants for you.

Specific. Stay away from making long, broad-focus, affirmations. It should state exactly what you want to motivate yourself to accomplish.

Positive. Your affirmations should be free of negative statements and words. Using negative words can contradict your purpose for the affirmation.

Emotional. Your affirmation should get you excited about where you're going or what you're trying to accomplish.

Short and sweet. If more than one sentence or 6 words is required, you should probably write more than one affirmation to cover the point.

Use your personal affirmations and visualizations to keep you motivated and with the right attitude. A bright, upbeat attitude will go a long way in helping you to stay optimistic.

Be Confident.

No one is perfect. We are all human and have flaws. Even the most successful people have flaws. Most have entertained the thought of not being good enough, smart enough, or strong enough to "finish."

But if you give in to those thoughts, you'll lose before you start. You have to believe in yourself, *especially* when you don't believe in yourself.

"If you have not confidence in self, you are twice defeated in the race of life." –
Marcus Garvey

So here's what you should do to build your confidence:

Recall your talents and skills. No matter how you're feeling, remind yourself of the things you excel at or the accomplishments you've achieved. Focusing on your great attributes will distract you from your perceived flaws and boost your self-esteem.

Know you are not alone. Everyone struggles with confidence. Some of us are better at hiding it than others, but we have all doubted ourselves at one point in life. You are not the first and you won't be the last. You are in great company.

Accept compliments. This one was very hard for me. I would always look for reasons to justify why I didn't deserve the compliment. Then a college friend called my attention to what I was doing. He said, "Sharon, just say 'thank you.'" If you're still uncomfortable, try giving a compliment back after you've accepted.

Walk the walk. There are tons of sayings for this one, such as "fake it 'til you make it" or "if it walks like a duck, and talks like a duck, it must be a duck." From your hygiene and dress to your posture, smile and eye contact, you can exude confidence in the way you carry yourself. If you know that you look like a confident, capable person, eventually you'll start to feel, act, talk and walk like it too.

Keep at it. Being confident isn't a one time achievement, it's a process. There will be days when you feel like you lost it completely and other days when you have enough to share with the world! So when it's low, take a deep breath, start at the top of this list until you build it again. Then share it with others!

Be Unwavering.

I remember as a child, seeing an image of a Chicagoan facing and leaning into a heavy, harsh wind. He was holding his coat rigidly across his chest with one hand and his hat fixed upon his head with the other. He was pressed, head first, directly into and against that wind. His entire body was leaning forward at a 45 degree angle as everything else, from newspapers to shopping carts, were blowing past him. Where ever it was that he was going, he was determined to get there. When I think of being unwavering, this is what I think of.

To waver means to feel or show doubt, or to hesitate. To be unwavering is to be firm, steady, unbendable or immovable.

As obstacles and challenges come your way, know that "this too shall pass" and that you are ready, prepared, and willing to overcome and move forward. Know that no matter what, you won't be blown away in the wind if you are determined to reach your destination.

So here are a few tips to keep you strong:

Believe in your success. Don't sell yourself short, and by all means don't let anybody else bring you down. Allow all the negativity to fly by in the wind.

When you know deep in your heart that this is something you want to do and you are willing to do everything it takes, press forward.

Believe in your capabilities. There are some people who really and truly do not have the skills required. But these same people *can learn*! Whether you take a class to polish your skills or teach yourself through reading, you can build your skills and capabilities to help you reach success.

Believe in you. No matter how bad the situation seems, believe in your success, believe in your capabilities, and believe in you. You deserve success. The fact that you took the time to define what success means to you, developed a route to get there, and now have prepared yourself to take action to make it real is proof that you deserve it.

Once you've determined your destination and purpose in life, you have to give it all you've got to make it real. As you go thru life, you'll undoubtedly encounter strong winds. But when you are certain, with all that is within you, that the course you are on is indeed the only course for you, don't waver... press forward.

Stick to your plan, stay focused and take action. Hold tight to your coat and hat, then press forward into the wind, head first.

Be Strategic.

Lastly, with your goal clearly in front of you, you need to be strategic. Having a *strategy* means that you have a long-term plan of action to reach your success. Being *strategic* means that you are ensuring that every step you take is aligned with your plan and that you are properly and effectively managing and utilizing your resources to help you get there.

Consider the video game Super Mario. His ultimate goal is saving the princess. To save the princess, Mario has to survive several smaller missions. Along the way, he has access to various resources to which will help him to achieve his mission. There are mushrooms that make him bigger or smaller, allow him to throw ice or move faster, or even give him a new life. There are flowers that allow him to throw fire and feathers that allow him to fly. Each mission requires different resources or skills to complete the tasks. But if you've ever played the game, or you're like me and just watched, you have to use those resources *at just the right time for just the right reason*. You need to know where to go to get the resource you need, when you need it. You also need to know how to use it most effectively.

So let's get back to your success. To know what resources you have available to you, you will need to work through your Personal S.W.O.T. Analysis (PSA). Your PSA is an inventory of your strengths, weaknesses, opportunities and threats. You goal with this information is to maximize your strengths, minimize your weaknesses, take advantage of your opportunities and eliminate your threats. In other words, your PSA helps you to identify your mushrooms, flowers and feathers, which are the skills, talents, and resources you need to reach your success… ensuring that every step you take is aligned with your master plan for success.

So there it is. Success is your target. Being in FOCUS will help you to stay motivated when the vision of your success gets distorted or blurry.

My Vision, My Plan, MY NOW

If you want to reach it, before you even take the first step towards it, you have to see it and you have to see it *clearly*. FOCUS.

- Be Fearless
- Be Optimistic
- Be Confident
- Be Unwavering
- Be Strategic

Sharon A. Myers

Sharon A. Myers is the President/CEO of Myers Technical Services, LLC, a management consulting and training company. She is also the Executive Director of Moovin4ward Presentations, a youth empowerment company that facilitates leadership and success workshops for high school and college students around the country. She is the co-developer of the **Journey to Success: Personal Success Strategic Plan (PSSP) Program**. She co-authored the program's companion book, *Mapping Your Journey to Success: Six Steps for Personal Planning*. Sharon is also the author of *Slumber Party*, a fictional story about young girls facing and overcoming girlhood pitfalls.

sharon@moovin4ward.com
www.Moovin4ward.com
www.Journey2Success.com

Part 2: My Plan

My Vision, My Plan, MY NOW

My Vision, My Plan, MY NOW

Chances, Choices, Change

Elethia Gay

For years I questioned past decisions. I wondered where I would be if I had chosen another route. Then my daughter was born and I realized I was exactly where I needed to be. I was a mom. There was no greater gift than giving birth. A couple years later, I saw an ad from Monster.com for a high school presenter. They were looking for public speakers who could speak to students from high schools and colleges around the nation. From that first day of training, once again I knew this was where I needed to be. Five years later, the "should of's" and "could ofs" are gone. This is my plan, my vision and my future and some lessons I learned along the way.

Tap Dance Lessons

"Kick, ball, change," "Kick, ball, change" "Kick, ball, change" were the instructions we received from our dance teacher. I was so excited to be a part of tap. As long as I could remember I wanted to be a tap dancer. When I finally had that chance at age 11, I was elated. It was about $4 a month for the classes. The only other requirement, arrive by 6 a.m. Now to someone less than a mile from the school, that would be fairly simple. However, I lived more than 10 miles from the school.

That meant I had to get up at 4:30 every morning just to get there in time. And I did... because I wanted to become the best tap dancer EVER!

Age 11 is also the year of "becoming." You're entering those teenage years. For some it can be a fun time or it can be a time of trying to figure things out. Who are my friends? What groups will I join? How will I survive these years without total embarrassment? For me, I just wanted to be accepted.

There was a girl. She was by far not the most popular girl for her great personality. In fact, to us girls she was a double threat. First, the boys loved her curves and her other developed body parts. Thus, she was stealing our boyfriends. Second, she was mean and big. We were scared of her. So we tried being her "friend" or avoiding her completely. I chose the friend route.

Since school began after 7:00am, I would go to her house after my train ride and eat breakfast most mornings. I noticed outside of school she seemed quite nice when you got to know her. Yet at school she became both mean and bossy. I hated her attitude shift. However, I thought becoming her nearest and dearest friend meant the behavior shifting would stop. Soon one or two times a week, for our breakfast meetings, turned into four and then five days per week. Before I knew it, I was skipping my tap lessons just to be her friend. In my heart, I wanted to tap but my head was telling me to be her friend. I would try to encourage her to go with me but she had no interest. After a month, I skipped so many classes that I fell far behind the other students.

Eventually, I started to regret my decision. Why was I was hanging out with this girl? Were we really friends? When I think back, we had little in common. I made the choice to give up tap, my dream at the time, just to be friends with her. In hindsight I realize I didn't have the best time with her. Selfishly I befriended her for my own benefit. I chose being accepted over pursuing my passion. Interestingly at the end of that year, she left our school.

An Opportunity in Law

It was my junior year of high school and I was part of Mr. S's mock trial program. It was a great effort on his part. He even had lawyers from one of the city's top law firms help with our practicing and preparation. I loved the mock trials. When I was a kid, my dad swore up and down that I needed to become a lawyer. I think it was my smart mouth but maybe he saw something else.

Being part of the mock trials taught me so much. I learned how to build a strong team, speak up for myself and gather my facts in order to build a strong argument. It was great practice for a future in law. And at the end of the trials, a student would be chosen to intern at the law firm.

Around this time, I found what I thought was my first love. I was 17. He was 18 and worked at one of the top financial firms in the World Trade Center. He was a total charmer. I both loved and hated to watch him work his magic with the ladies. However, I loved being with him because he allowed me to come out of my shell.

Shortly before the end of the school year we broke up for the sixth time. I was upset that he didn't call or spend time with me or seem committed in any way. However, I was in love. You could not tell me anything different.

It was the end of the mock trials and it was time to choose the intern at this top law firm in the city. Anyone in their right mind saw the opportunity this presented. The internship provided an experience that was priceless. Out of the four people on our team, they chose me! I should have jumped at the opportunity and at first, I did. However, another internship opportunity opened up with the Port Authority. With this internship you were randomly chosen to work at one of two locations, LaGuardia Airport or the World Trade Center. My hopes were that I would get a chance to work at the World Trade Center.

Given the options of possibly seeing my love or practicing my craft, I chose the Port Authority internship. I cannot remember the excuse given to the attorneys who dedicated months to choosing the right person. It doesn't matter anymore. A couple weeks after rejecting the law firm opportunity, the decision came down from the Port Authority. I was being sent to LaGuardia Airport for the summer.

I made a choice that changed the course of my career. I was so lost and insecure in myself that I made a choice I would soon regret. No one coerced me. I gave my power away. Sometimes we have the power to choose and sometimes we are chosen. It is when we are chosen that our egos speak the loudest. It tells us that we still have a choice. We can say "yes" or we can say "no." However, in this case I followed my fears and not my heart which led me to say, "No" to the law firm internship. My heart was not following my love. My choice was not made for love. I feared **not** being loved. I feared being alone. Sometimes we overlook opportunities that are presented because we are afraid of the unknown, it just seems too easy, or we need some outside validation to move forward.

When this happens we need to remember that there are times when we are chosen. Reflect, meditate, have faith and then revisit your plan. You will know when to say, "Yes."

Starting Anew

There are three things this girl dreamed about growing up... going to college, getting married, having kids and being a successful business woman. Okay that's four. I am ambitious. My dreams and goals were not only based on what I wanted, but they were also based on what I did not want or worse - what might happen if they were not accomplished. While there's nothing wrong with knowing what you do not want, when you make decisions based on what you fear, your decisions can be rushed and often faulty.

First there was college. College was a decision based on my dreams and my goals. It was the key to success. College was also my ticket out of the "hood." Plus, every rich and successful business woman attended college, at least that's how it appeared on TV. College wasn't simply a way - it was the ONLY way.

Then there was marriage. To me, marriage was the cure all for bad relationships, loneliness and cheating men. My only access to healthy marriages came from TV where marriage meant security. It meant protection. It meant blissful happiness. It meant forever. I didn't have real life role models who helped me understand the mechanics of making a relationship work, let alone a marriage. It wasn't until later that I learned marriage is more than the vows. It's 2Corinthians plus more. It's not meant to be perfect or a denial of whom you are. Marriage is who you are plus whom they are and what you two become. Becoming is the best part. It is every minute detail of a relationship - nothing more, nothing less. It is not easily defined. It is a creation built by two partners with no set of instructions upon a mutual foundation. However, if you do not take time to truly understand what marriage is, who you are and what a relationship is, it can become nothing more than a routine and a safety net.

At age 20 I still held on to the ideologies I found on TV as to what marriage was. I did not know about foundational elements of making any type of relationship work. I wanted someone to love me. That's it. I simply liked what a relationship looked like. Whether it was laughing, holding hands, or cuddling, these external displays of affection were my definitions of love.

I applied such stringent rules to the word m-a-r-r-i-a-g-e. Marriage meant total compromise. It meant forgetting your passions and desires to be a "wife." It meant your husband was perfect regardless of any cheating or relapses in judgment. He was the save-all and cure-all. Worshiping together, communicating regularly, being around like minded individuals, sharing in each other's passions didn't mean a thing in my view of marriage.

I was still wrapped up in this fantasy at age 25 when a friend said, "Get married already! What are you waiting for?" Though it was against my better judgment, we did it anyway. We loved each other (which later I learned was based on fear), we were always together and we did not argue. That was enough. At least that's what I thought.

A month before our marriage, we went to counseling. At the time it just seemed like a formality. After all, I had my mind made up. I was going to marry this man. It was during our first session that the first sign appeared. We were discussing the things we liked and what we needed to work on in our relationship. At the end of the session our counselor said, "If you wanted to marry right now, I would not be able to marry you." So we went home that night, discussed (compromised) those things we disagreed on and a month later we married.

After three years, I knew we needed counseling. We were leading separate lives. I was volunteering, attending church and bible study regularly. I was outgoing yet I felt stifled when we were with others. I wanted to dance at parties and engage in lively table talk. I wanted to attend the "married people" parties. I was curious as to what other relationships looked like. Overall, I wanted to be seen and heard. I wanted to join in the game of life. While I felt compelled to address our differences, we never went back to counseling. We swept it under the rug. We compromised.

After eight years of marriage and eleven years of compromise, we split. I forgot who I was and I felt I was unfairly asking him to become someone he was not intended to be. You can read all the books, listen to numerous speakers and take years of counseling on how to have a successful marriage. What I learned from my experience was how to face my truth. It is so easy to blame someone else for our shortcomings and failures. Yet, how many of us admit to ourselves the part we play in the outcome. What are our challenges? What baggage do we bring to the relationship? How do we pursue our personal and spiritual growth?

What is your truth about who you are? We must show and tell others how we want to be treated. We must discern our boundaries and communicate them to others. We must decide that we have the power to be happy by looking within and stop expecting someone else to make us happy, to bring us joy.

Choices Determine Our Path

Our choices have such an influence on our outcome in life. Plans change and visions are altered based on the choices we make. When we allow outside influences to define who we are, we lose sight of what's important. We end up choosing to chase a dream that doesn't belong to us. This is not to encourage one to avoid making choices. Making a choice is an inevitable task. It's essential to living. Some are almost involuntary. If you ever reach a crossroads and don't know what to choose, simply ask "Am I following my heart or am I following my fears or someone else's plan?"

Every day we are faced with choices. These choices can be amongst several options or alternatives. Some of our choices are small and some are big and impactful. What do you want out of life? Who will your decisions impact? It seems complicated yet it's very simple. The question is not whether the choice is right or wrong. It is the path it leads us down. Brace yourself, choices are an everyday thing. Regret is the lowest form of respecting your right to choose. Live through your choice and if it does not lead you to where you want to go - make different choices!

ELETHIA GAY

Elethia Gay is an experienced life coach, author, speaker and personal trainer. After receiving her MBA from Mercer University, she completed extensive training in personal life management and organizational behavior. Her areas of expertise include: Diversity and Inclusion, The Whole Brain model, 7 Habits of Highly Effective People, Managerial Skills, Effective Communication Skills and Color Analysis. Elethia's expertise in brand management allowed her to build over 10 years of marketing and advertising experience with brands like Domino's Pizza and Ford. She took that branding expertise to her personal clients and helps them reinvent their brand through personalized image strategies. Her personal branding techniques focus on mind and body because she believes your personal brand is more than what you see. In 2008, she began a national speaking career that has enabled her to share her expertise with over 10,000 students each year. In her personal time, she serves as a Bullying Prevention Trainer with NCCY.org. Elethia also enjoys teaching fitness classes, designing a new t-shirt line, and serving on grass root campaigns that promote economic independence for women.

Contact Info:

F: facebook.com/alexanderqimagegroup
T: @aqimagegroup
W: aqimagegroup.com
E: info@aqimagegroup.com

My Vision, My Plan, MY NOW

The Unicycle: When the Ordinary Just Won't Do

Rodney Burris

It's 8am and your morning route to work has miraculously gone as planned. There were no wardrobe malfunctions or car troubles. Even the kind people at Dunkin Donuts remembered to put the right amount of sugar and cream in your coffee. As you listen to your favorite morning radio show, laughing at their corny jokes, you turn the corner and your heart drops – TRAFFIC JAM! Your eyes dart from the clock to the traffic and back again, until you finally come to grips; you will not be able to take your normal route. This is an all too familiar scene. It happens to the best of us. In fact, this can often be a painful reminder of other areas of our lives. We often have plans, directions, or routes for our lives (whether we designed them or not), and they don't always pan out. But the hardest decision for many of us is to break cycles that have become normal, comfortable, and psychological engrained, even when we know they no longer work.

It is often said that we need to break cycles in our lives; cycles of pain, failure, and non-success. Why is it so hard? As crazy as this may sound, I recently spent a lot of time researching unicycles, after having seen a performer ride one in Baltimore's Inner Harbor. The way the rider moved was mesmerizing, as if he could simply defy the rules of nature and physics at will. So I knew unicycle-riding was something that I needed to look into, if simply to scratch my own curiosity... and maybe build up the courage to try it one day myself. But my research showed me that unicycles can teach us a lot about navigating life itself, especially when life throws you a curve ball.

Learn From the Past

Let's start with the obvious. It should be no surprise that the word unicycle shares the same root meaning as the word unique: "uni". It is meant to signify singularity, individuality, and being "the only". Anyone who has ever seen a unicycle in use can definitely attest to it's unique status. And one of the reasons why the unicycle is considered unique is because it can do something that other manual modes of transportation often do not; it can cycle backwards.

Let's take a bicycle for example. By physical design, bicycles are only designed to move in the same direction, unless it is physically/manually acted upon with force (squeezing the brakes). And even with this motion, the cycle cannot move backwards. Reversing is not an option. As fast as a motorcycle is, have you ever seen its rider moving it backwards? It is the most awkward, clumsy, precarious walk possible, and is normally only done to back up a few feet in order to park, or so that the rider can change direction and once again move forward. Even in life, when we notice that we have taken a wrong route, we may try to reverse the motion and take the cycle back, trying to redo some past situation in our lives by using the same vehicle that got us there. At best, the wheels will spin and we get nowhere. Even when we try to stop to avoid further danger, a quick stop could cause us to fall and cause injury. However, just as easily as the unicycle moves forward, the direction can be reversed and you can retrace your steps.

It's impossible to turn back the hands of time and redo a part of your life. What is done is done. Many of us spend an inordinate amount of lives wishing we had a magical time machine that could get rid of mistakes and pains. Maybe the trauma of being hurt as a child or in past relationships could be avoided. Maybe we could do things differently and cause our credit score to be closer to 800. Unfortunately, we can't change the past. But we can redefine it. Instead of treating it as a source of pain, treat it as a wellspring of advice. It is important to learn from the past. We are destined to repeat history if we don't learn from it. But we've all heard that statement and understand it completely. The question is why don't many of us learn from it?

Let's go back to our analogy. The unicycle can move in reverse, but the most uncomfortable thing is the rider cannot turn his body around to see. In reverse, you can't control what you see. In the same way, traveling back to our past is uncomfortable, because we can't control what we see. Often times, we don't even want to see it again, because it may elicit pain that we dread revisiting. So we repress the past and cycle as far away from it as possible, and as fast we can. But no matter how uncomfortable it is to go in reverse, no matter how much you feel that moving backwards is a waste of time, it is tantamount to success. Revisiting the past may be painful, but it is a constant reminder that we can avoid recreating trauma, if we learn from the past and avoid pitfalls.

Find a Support System

Although the prefix *uni* in the word unicycle implies that you must ride alone, almost all websites that provide riding tips suggest that you have a support system in case you fall. Though there is only one person riding the cycle, several people should be standing there to support you and keep you moving in the right direction. Likewise, practically every course on business and financial success, every self-help book, and every spiritual or religious group have a principle that encourages us to seek advice. You are no doubt familiar with many of the normal colloquialisms. There's strength in numbers. Together we stand and divided we fall. The list goes on.

In our own personal growth, it is important to surround ourselves with people who can provide wisdom and support. The famous author, John Donne, said it poignantly when he penned the words, "No man is an island, entire of itself." Growth cannot happen successfully unless we have a counsel of friends, loved ones, and even professionals that help us navigate the difficult times. We need advice and encouragement from others. Without these things, we are destined to fall off-course -- off the cycle -- and cause psychological harm. Even though your support system may not be available financially, it is the intangible, emotional support that undergirds us the most. The easiest way to feel defeated is to ride this cycle of life alone. When you fall (AND YOU WILL!), you will experience dejection and focus only on your pain and scars. Your support system will be there to catch you. And even when they can't keep you from falling, they will serve as a constant reminder that you can get back up and still be a winner.

Create Balance

One of the toughest things about a unicycle is that there is no handle bar to rest on, maintain balance, or change direction. Your body must stay in an upright position. Every motion must be calculative and planned. Yes, it takes enormous abdomen strength, and you must continuously grab from within. That's what personal trainers refer to as *pulling from the core*. In the same respect, you must reach down into the core of who you are in order to create balance in your life.

Growing up, I didn't consider myself a good bicycle rider until I could ride with no hands. The handle bars and outstretched arms allow you to spread your body weight out over the length of the bike, which gives you great control. Think about it: How much more stable are you when you are laying down (outstretched) than standing up on one foot? We always blame it on our "balance," but actually it's quite simple; being stretched out increases our center of gravity (ability to control our own body); being up on one foot means that you have to balance yourself differently than you would normally. Riding a unicycle takes this concept, and amplifies it to a dozen times over. It means that your center of balance, your sense of control, is significantly thrown off. You are in a new situation, (having to) do new things you are not comfortable, and you have not found that new sense of stability. This is hard for any of us.

Being away from your center of gravity makes it easy to hurt yourself or be hurt from others, because you aren't in as much control as you think. We are out of "balance." In the 80's and 90's, diet programs said the way to lose weight is to cut fat. Today the same programs say cutting carbs is the way to go. At the end of the day, every elderly person will tell you, "everything in moderation." Many of our problems come because we choose diets, lifestyles, and thought patterns that lean more to one side than the other; we are left out of balance.

In that respect, it's probably true that most people are missing balance in their lives. We work too much and cause stress at home. We may spend more time with our kids or our friends than we do nurturing our spouse. We may spend all our money on bills and retirement accounts and never spend money on a much-needed vacation to refuel. We run to this meeting and that meeting, but never run on the treadmill to stay fit.

Let's learn to slow down and create balance. The Leaning Tower of Pisa may be astonishing, but what makes it famous is that most buildings would have collapsed. Don't collapse. It may seem easier to focus on one thing more than another, but find balance and watch your stress level drop.

Take the Unconventional Route

I can hear you saying, "enough with the unicycle analogy!" I mean let's be honest; why ride a unicycle when you can ride a bicycle? The bike is easier. It takes much more abdomen strength to control and balance a unicycle. Then again, why ride a bicycle when you can ride a motorcycle? As the name implies, it has a motor. You expend less energy and the seat is more comfortable. While you're at it, why not use a car to get to your destination? It's much safer than a motorcycle. I'm glad you asked. All of these alternative paths involve doing what is easy, comfortable, and safe. In order to reach our fullest potential, we can't afford to always play it safe. You have to take calculated risks. Sometimes we are forced to, sometimes it is by choice.

Recently, I met with a financial advisor to start investing in the stock market. Before he chose what stocks to invest in, he had me fill out a form that asked me whether I'm willing to risk greater financial loss, with the hopes of making more money in the long run. What a life lesson! I could play it safe and guarantee a small return. Or I can be more aggressive, unconventional, and take more risk in order to make the most of my money. In the words of a famous hip hop artist, "Scared money don't make money." Don't get me wrong; I'm not giving financial advice, but the principle is parallel. Most people will choose the path of least resistance, because we prefer less work and stress. But if you're going to be successful, you have to be a trailblazer and chart your own course. No matter how scary it is, get out of your comfort zone.

The yield is often much greater. The famous poet, Robert Frost, wrote in one of his most heralded works, "Two roads diverged in the woods, and I – I took the one less traveled by, and that has made all the difference." Learning how to be comfortable in situations where most people would struggle is an invaluable asset, and one that will serve you well in life, both personally and professionally. The unicycle exemplifies the gaining of this skillset.

I'm sure you've read more in this chapter about unicycles than you ever thought you'd read – or want to read. But even if you throw the information away, treasure the lesson. Don't be that person who runs from the past, going through life alone, using everyone else's path as their own blueprint for success.

I once heard a commencement speech delivered by Bill Cosby that changed my life. He told a story about one night early in his career. He was hired to perform a comedy set at a club. Nobody knew him. He had never been the featured act at a venue this large. Fear gripped him and he bombed. No one laughed. As he ended the first half of his act and walked off stage, the club manager who hired him scolded him. He asked Bill, "who was that on stage?" Bill looked perplexed, because it was clear that the manager knew it was he who just performed. Maybe it was the makings of a cruel joke. Cosby answered, "It was me." The club manager disagreed and said that whoever the comedian was that bombed the first half needs to stay backstage after intermission. Before walking away, the manager informed him, "the world is waiting for the real Bill Cosby to show up."

You are no different. The entire universe is waiting for the real you to show up. Travel back to the past in order to learn from it. Surround yourself with positive, caring, successful people – no matter how you define success. Create balance in your life to reduce stress. And most importantly, get out of your comfort zone and seek your own path. Tailor it specifically for you to actualize your full potential. The world is waiting.

RODNEY BURRIS

Educator, National Speaker, Youth and Family Advocate, and Entrepreneur; these are some of the words used to describe Rodney Burris. In addition to a wide range of career experience, the common thread among all his ventures is a strong desire to strengthen communities.

Mr. Burris holds a BA in Psychology from the Johns Hopkins University and an MS in Management of Nonprofit Agencies from Capella University. He is deeply rooted in neighborhood empowerment and has tutored struggling students, encouraged area leaders to become more involved in the community, and reconnected fathers with their children, advising them on parenting and life skills. Rodney is also an avid promoter of business development and entrepreneurship. His combined knowledge of non-profit experience and business-startup has been used to assist scores of interested learners.

RodneyBurris@mail.com
www.RodneyBurris.com
@RodneyCBurris

Do you have your P.H.D?

Mark Wiggins

When I feel like I have lost the desire to chase my dreams or to complete the simplest of tasks that will help me reach my goals, I sometimes find it necessary to go back to a familiar place... a place that reminds me of what is possible when you have passion for your purpose. I had to go to that place very recently; when I sat down to write my chapter for this book.

This didn't come easy for me, because I wasn't motivated to sit down and write.

Why? Because I am a speaker, and simply put, I would rather speak than write.

Yet I realize that thinking this is just an excuse, and that's when I go to my "familiar place."

And where is that place that I go to get my passion or to level up the excitement for doing new things and taking chances?

I go to the gym...the basketball court more specifically.

When I go to the gym, I am reminded of a time where I learned that if I worked hard and gave my full effort, I would see results. It was the basketball court where a passion to play basketball; the hunger to learn new skills, and the drive to win bounded together to create the player and eventually the speaker that I am today.

Now I hear you thinking, "Well Speaker Man, I didn't play sports when I was a kid, or have any athletic ability, so how will I get these skills?"

My response to that is, "So what?"

Your story may be different, but I use sports as MY backdrop to get MY point across, and that point is simple: even if you have never played sports, been to college, started a business, or written a book, **everyone** has passion about something.

We all innately have the hunger to achieve great things and to experience the emotion that comes when you are fully engaged in something.

So I believe if you want to have success, you must have your P.H.D.

I am not saying you need to go back to college for more years, what I am saying is that you need to get your **Passion**, **Hunger** and **Drive** back. Passion has been described as a strong and barely controllable emotion. I believe that passion is the answer to the questions: "What do you feel strongly about? What would your work for even if you didn't get paid?

I have a passion for helping young people, so when I am engaged with them, I am in my wheelhouse. I give them all I have and when I am finished working with or speaking, I am drained, literally wiped out; but it is a great type of tired.

In my free time, I coach youth basketball. Recently, I was coaching a middle school team at a private Christian school. It a growing program, but the players were lacking that "thing", that passion for the game and as a result, they were not a good team.

Before I took the job I told the Director that I was different type of coach; that I always drove my kids to become better, and I would not let them accept less than their best. I can remember one time where I was deep in the game and coaching hard and really motivating my kids. I was sweating more than them. After the game the Athletic Director of the other team approached me and said, "Wow you sure are passionate about the game!" She was trying to be nice and not say that I was a mad man on the sidelines. But I couldn't help myself.

When you are passionate about what you want to do or to achieve, you give it your all because you are fully engaged and present in what is going on.

What about you? Can you answer the big question; what are you passionate about? If you cannot answer that question, then I suggest that you go back to that "place" and reflect. Maybe you cannot go there physically, but in your mind, think back to that time where you were excited about getting up and being engaged in something, maybe it was a project that you started but then got sidetracked with life, ran up against some obstacles, got discouraged and walked away from it thinking you would never complete it. Maybe it's time to look at it again.

While reading this book and getting different angles of how to create your vision, and how to claim your "NOW", think about those things that motivated you.

When on your path, one of the first things to deal with is lost motivation. Keeping yourself motivated and moving toward goals is a very tough thing; you have barriers and obstacles that come across your path. Obstacles like self-doubt, haters, lost enthusiasm, fear, and the others, will make a great exit ramp of your journey to success. They will cause you to lose your passion, hunger and drive at the same time. When you are faced with these challenges, it is at that time you must ask the question, "WHAT IS MY WHY?" Why did I start this in the first place?

When you do that, you will be able to remember your passion and will again be motivated to get off the bench and back in to the starting line up of life. Your vision of what you want to do or be has its roots in your Passion. If you have lost your passion you lose focus on your vision.

Hunger

Hunger is one of the primary things that push you to do something; you cannot ignore the signs of hunger. There is a old story about a lion and a gazelle in the plains of Africa, it is said that every morning a lion wakes up thinking that he just be faster than the slowest gazelle in order for him to eat, and every morning a gazelle wakes up and thinks that he must be just a bit faster than the slowest gazelle or he will die. That's motivation driven by hunger. Maslow writes in his Hierarchy of Needs that hunger is ranked second in the list of needs required for life.

Do you have the hunger for your Now? This type of hunger is what you feel if you don't reach your goals. Hunger will motivate you to do something to satisfy that urge. In this case your hunger for success will keep you doing what you need to do to work. You must have a way to get what you want to satisfy that hunger. When lions stalk their prey, there is a plan that they execute. When the plan is executed, the result is dinner. So what is your plan, what will you do make sure you satisfy that hunger for success, or achieve your goal? Hunger is *your* well thought out plan. Remember though, the lion hunts often, they must eat daily, so you will have to work on your goals every day.

Make sure your plan will allow you to satisfy that hunger daily; something must always be done. Either you are chasing it, or its running from you…the only constant in this equation is that you must have a plan, or your fate will be left to others.

Drive

Drive can be explained as one of those intangible things that cannot be taught. You see this in business and in sports a great deal. Those who have drive are the most successful. They might not be the most talented or the smartest, but something about the desire to achieve that just will not be denied propels them to success.

Drive is a choice, either you have it or you do not, you cannot "somewhat" have drive. A great example of drive was Steve Jobs. His desire was not to make Apple a major player in the world of technology, but THE major force.

That goal took drive, a tenacity that would not stop until he reached his goal.

I have a philosophy that I believe will help you has you evaluate and prepare to get our P.H.D. back. The formula is simple MTXE is the formula for success. I believe in that philosophy so much that I wrote a book about it.

The title is "MTXE: The Formula for Success"

Let me define MTXE. M is for mental. This is where you set your goals and dream about what you want in life. T stands for toughness, you will need to have a certain toughness to deal with all the challenges you will face, those from outside forces and those from within. X stands for Xtreme. You know the quote, "If you do the same thing over and over and expect a different result, its called insanity." Xtreme. What we do day-to-day are the things that are normally in our comfort zone. Trying something totally different to achieve a goal would be Xtreme.

The last letter is E. E stands for EFFORT. What will you *do* to achieve your goal? It can be described as the action step, the doing portion the equation.

Drive is what you must have NOW in order to achieve your success. It will not do any good just to think dream, or plan about what you want to NOW, you must have that drive to go get it NOW. Drive is what you must DO NOW to achieve your goals.

Now that you know what PHD is, you should be asking, "How do I get my PHD?

Well I'm glad you asked. I will give you 5 steps to getting Your Passion, Your Hunger, and Your Drive back so you can energize Your Vision, Your Plan, Your NOW.

Step 1

Find your Why.

Go back in time and remember what it was that got you so fired up in the first place. Remember the end goal…What was the vision?

What were the steps, actions, or situations that lead you to the place where you said, THIS IS ME! I totally believe in this.

If you are not sure what it is that makes you smile or causes you to get energized about what you love; then, start looking at every part of your life, the things you do, the things you like and if you could do it for free you would do.

That is most likely your passion.

Losing your WHY happens over time; again, sometimes life creeps in, we get distracted with what we believe to be more important things to do. Routines often cause us to lose our why. When we do things over and over and over again, we find a way to make it easy so we use less emotion and energy to get it done. In psychology it's called creating "schemas". Schemas are mental short cuts to thinking about things, or taking the path of least emotional resistance; it can be done in our sleep. This ease of doing things will put you into to the zone of comfort and create a lack of energy. Remember you must have Passion for your purpose that will give you the strength to endure.

Step 2

Visualize your success.

I have a speaker friend who always says you should spend 5 minutes a day in your success. He believes that when you take the time to see yourself as you dream you would be, it will help you stay motivated. In the program that I helped Co-create with Sharon A. Myers, called *Journey to Success* we speak about the positive effects of visualization. This is the practice of not just seeing your success, but engaging all your senses in that success. You should smell it, taste it, hear it, feel it and see it. So when you do your visualization be very descriptive and include details, details, and details. The more descriptive you are the more likely you will get your motivation and your PHD back, and you will find things coming into your space, that is called the Law of Attraction. This law states that we draw into our life what we dream about, fantasize and focus on the most. So if you find yourself not feeling the passion for your purpose, try visualizing your desired results. People say that perception is reality, therefore if you want to change your reality, change your perception...5 minutes a day.

Step 3

Find birds with the same feather.

The saying goes, "Birds of a feather flock together."

So when they flock together, they have something in common. You must surround yourself with people who are like-minded. Meet with people who are like you so you can stay motivated. I used to speak for a national speaking company that met every 6 months for training and certification. Now that does not sound like much, but when you are in a room with 250 of the best speakers in the country, you were forced to be on top of your game when you showed up.

Not that is was a competition, but you knew if you called yourself a professional speaker, you needed to be a professional.

What I remembered most was the way I felt when I left the training. I was recharged and ready to speak to whomever and where ever I could. The positive synergy that was created by being around other folks like me helped me through the challenging times when I questioned myself as a speaker and trainer. There is a reason there are so many associations and organizations, because they know that when you are with like-minded people you can express yourself to others that understand what you are going through. Often times we quit right before our breakthrough happens. Having the support group with that same "feather" is what you need to uplift you and keep you going.

Step 4

Do something daily.

It is hard to measure success because success is personal. However, you can measure your progress. You need to be doing something each day towards your goals. If you have your plan laid out, and you do something towards that goal, you achieve that goal.

When you stay motivated, you experience success often, and when you experience success often, you achieve more. But you must do something daily.

My old college Coach Michael Scrano taught me that that you must always work to improve never work to maintain. What that meant for us back during practice in college was simple, if you have to be there every day and practice why not do something to get better? Same applies to you, if you are going to do something during the day, why not do something towards your goal, why not use your PHD to make your vision, you plan your now a reality? The answer to the old African riddle of how can you eat an elephant, is simply this...one bite at a time.

Step 5

Evaluate your progress.

Again, success is personal. Since it is personal there is no real standard way to measure it. What you consider to be a success someone else may consider a failure. I often say, that if you give others the power to define your success, then you give them power to define your failures. I do not know about you but I am not willing to let others that power.

In my book *Permission to Succeed*, the only person who needs to give permission is you. I talk about how not to look to others for permission to do thing that you want to do, but rather to look internally and empower yourself to do it.

The same goes for getting your P.H.D. As you get on your journey to success you need to have your plan and your vision so that there is a Now. We get so focused on the "doing" that we don't take time to reward ourselves or to adjust our course of action. We make great plans then we just go.

But what if things change? What if the tasks seem to be so large we feel like we are not making progress?

These are barriers to success and must be handled. These are energy leaks and take away your passion. You get discouraged and might want to give up. In order to combat that, make time to evaluate your progress, see what has worked, what didn't and make the adjustment. When you take time to look back and see that you have been more successful than you have given yourself credit, you will get that passion back, and with that, the hunger to obtain more success. Then, the drive will help you get off the bench and back in to the starting lineup of life. So let's review my 5 steps to getting your P.H.D back:

1. Remember your WHY
2. Visualize your success
3. Find birds with the same feather
4. Do something daily
5. Evaluate your progress

Motivation is an external pushing force and must be repeated to get you going. Inspiration is a pulling force that comes from within.

However you need both motivation and inspiration to achieve your goals. Getting your PHD is not an easy process, and it takes focus and a "want to" attitude. Therefore, getting your PHD is a choice. The question is, will you make it? Because if you do, as you create your vision and create your plan, you will be ready to get to YOUR NOW.

> *"Passion for your purpose will give you the endurance to finish"*

MARK W. WIGGINS

Mark "The Speaker Man" Wiggins, an International speaker, trainer, author and entrepreneur is the CEO of Xtreme Effort Speaking. He has held lead-ership and management positions within several national retail companies, such as Foot Locker, Eddie Bauer, and Levi Strauss & Co. He has trained corporate, community, and association leaders in the Washington, DC area on the topics of customers, leadership and human performance.

He is the author of *Permission to Succeed: the Only Person Who Needs to Give it is You*; *MTXE the Formula for Success*; and more.

RAW

Audrey Stolfi

My struggle began with an emotionally absent mother, a drug-dealing uncle, and the only two people who loved me unconditionally, died of cancer. I knew early on failure was not an option. I come from a long line of survivors and entrepreneurs, so it's in my blood to excel and to exceed the expectations of my ancestors.

Being a determined overachiever and staying focused on personal and career goals has been the fiber of my character. There have been some delays in my journey. At times, I had to make a conscious decision to postpone or stall for reasons beyond my control; like a turbulent marriage or sheer exhaustion. But I always kept in mind that my path waits for me; patiently. The path waits for you but the opportunities don't. I'm not saying you won't get any other opportunities; but for me it delayed my journey to accomplish my potential. I always tell people "I still have so much more to do," even though it is not clear what these things are. But what is clear with every completed goal it frees up time for a charity or another personal goal which can turn into an opportunity for growth.

Take the time to enrich your life by contributing towards charitable organizations. They are always looking for volunteers and there are a variety of foundations, religious organizations, sports leagues or awareness groups looking for passionate and skilled people to get involved.

Getting involved for causes I believe in is what keeps me humble and grateful for all my blessings. It also validates my capabilities and character traits that have been defined by my work ethic. At times it translates into being controlling or being a bitch. But if at the end the objective is met, then I won't apologize for being assertive and I don't take it personal when I'm misunderstood.

In life we have to filter people and this is called quality control. The people you want to surround yourself with are the people who are not afraid to be honest with you and who will uplift you. These people add to your life by teaching you valuable lessons without tearing you down.

They demonstrate an emotional investment in your life and consistently prove their value; you can be your most vulnerable, transparent, and raw in their presence.

They will remind you of your worth, your potential, your path. For me these are a handful of very influential allies and their positive transcendence in my life has shaped my being. They are my support system. Since, I have very little immediate family and some have nothing positive to contribute; I made a decision to outperform all the low expectations from the shadow of family who imposed their status quo mentality. For me every milestone is a defining moment. Success comes in different levels, depends on the person and the cultural parameter. Success can also come from failure and until you are dead there is always something you can do. No matter the losses, failures, or disappointments- as long as you are breathing you have an opportunity to turn it around. Never give up.

Recently, I took my kids to Hershey Park on a three day pass that included tickets to the Milton Hershey museum. In touring the museum I learned that Milton Hershey had several failures before his success and legacy. It holds true that you need to do whatever it takes to materialize your vision, be consistent and invest as many hours necessary to secure your future. By sacrificing the incidentals you make a conscious decision to commit to your dream. Once progress starts reaping rewards you will realize how meaningless it is when you look back at the bigger picture. There are decisions in which you will have to make that will require precision and strategy.

Your vision is an authentic and pure idea, do your best not to waiver from the original concept.

When I take on a project, I am aware of the goal and how to accomplish it. My decisions are strategic and confident. I work with a variety of governmental agencies and deal with different interpretations of building codes and regulatory procedures and in my line of work, time is money. My services can be easily replaced if a project is not handled expeditiously. In every project I keep my integrity and character in tact while performing for others. Over the years I have learned to ask for help and in a lot of instances it is best to have resources to tap into if you need the assistance in areas of weakness or vulnerability. I was faced with this dilemma when my business was at its busiest, my kids had just returned to school and there was a gap in my time schedule between the end of the school day and my arrival at home. No matter how much you plan and prepare there is always going to be a variable or obstacle that you will have to overcome in order to maintain your objective. I had to tap into my support system to find a solution that would benefit both my children without sacrificing their quality of life. I have noticed that the only sacrifice that suffers is the time you get to spend with your children and sometimes it's a decision that has to be made for the greater good of their welfare. These are the decisions and sacrifices we make to better our lives, in hopes to leave a legacy for the future of your loved ones. Don't focus on the lack; learn to appreciate the haves. Maybe one day my kids will understand and appreciate the valuable lessons learned from watching me hustle.

My success was simple; I started a business in my late twenties and have been fortunate to reinvent and evolve with it. It empowers me to understand that I can make my future fruitful and prominent as long as I continue to invest in my vision. We are the master of our own Destiny. I heard this saying from a client who always encouraged and challenged me not to become complacent. "Comfortable people get lazy, competitive people perform," he would say. I have had many people in my life who have been an influence, one influential and life changing person was my uncle Jose Jaramillo who owns Papelesa Cia. Ltda, S.A by his acts, he has demonstrated great discipline, performance and will power. His works and success have proven that there is no limit to where your hard work can take you. Having a strong work ethic is your calling card. Make sure with every project or opportunity you leave this mark behind because the imprint you leave is your reputation.

As a woman in an industry where the glass ceiling had to be broken, I can tell you the struggle is the fire that roars inside of me, the hustle that I dance to every day. My clients can confirm that my diligence and determination is why they have continued to hire me. My personality is strong and intense but it's transparent and very simple to understand.

Once you arrive at the door step of your definition of success make sure to savor the moment but at the same time, one up it. There is no limit as to how far you can go, but you are the only one that can decide how far. In business the decisions are how fast you grow, when to expand your growth and what financial decisions need to be made to maintain what was implemented. This is the part of success that can breed greed. It is wise to remain a humble realist and hesitate from being self-serving. Do your best to maintain humility and remember how much sacrifice it took to get to the door step of success. You can define who you are by not subsiding to the material; rather define yourself by the immaterial. Think of it as spiritual transformation rather than physical. Always meet the needs rather than the wants. Money is not the root of all evil, it's the handler.

If you know you go crazy with money then treat it the way you would a family member who you know will hit you up for a loan; avoid it! Set aside your expenses and whatever is left over send to an annuity or seek advice from a reputable financial advisor for guidance. Out of site is out of mind.

I can testify from experience as to how fast wealth can be lost, it took me 10 years of hard work to gain and it took two years to lose. It is scarier to experience these types of losses when you are older; I am now forty and on my third company. The difference is I have a lot more experience in the do's and don'ts which make a really great business manual. It makes you hyper vigilant in your everyday operating procedures. You no longer have the luxury of wasting time; every opportunity is met with vigor, because this might be your last chance to fight for your dream. The world does not know lack, it only responds to acts.

If you do not perform you do not grow. It is only when you are raw that you can grow in the challenges; it's in growth that you meet your potential.

Growth is a healthy part of life and the decision to want to perform can only come from you. Whatever your goal, whether it's financial, career, personal or material it can only be realized by performance. I hope my testimony helps you create a road map to your future and motivates, you to want your dreams and goals to come true. The future does not have an expiration date and by continuing to work towards it you get to be the author of what is written in it. Think of it as a painting; the more colors you add the more vibrant the painting becomes, but always remember it started as a blank canvas. I am excited for the next chapter in my life and feel very blessed to be able to share my failures and successes with you. Always remember that neither of these are terminal.

AUDREY STOLFI

Audrey Stolfi is a seasoned entrepreneur; she has owned several companies and has worked with top construction and development firms. She is the owner of Expedite It Permit Processing Company in Washington, DC. She was recently featured in the Loudoun Times Mirror for her humanitarian effort to assist the victims of Hurricane Sandy.

You can follow her on twitter at **@dnastolfi** or connect with her on LinkedIn. For more information on RAW, send an email to **info@expediteitcompany.com**

My Vision, My Plan, MY NOW

The Chronicles of "X"

Xavier Smith

My name is Xavier Smith, and I am the one that is known for being happy to be alive! It is a part of who I am and as a matter of fact, people often finish the statement before I do. However, it goes beyond the simple phrase that is used as part of my motto. Hopefully after reading this chapter you will discover the deep, true and real meaning behind the words, "I am happy to be alive!"

I will do my best to paint a true and accurate picture of who I was, where I have come from, and the path of excellence I am on now! Some believe that you are shaped by the events that happen in one's life. I happen to agree with that statement. It is my hope that you will understand that regardless of where you come from, or who you used to be, or what path you are on at this very moment, you can start from where you are now, and get better (improve) from there! My purpose for writing this is to be a positive IMPACT and speak for those who are not ready to speak up for themselves, to be an INSPIRATION to those still stuck on the fence of mediocrity, and to let the world know that no matter who you are, we all have room for IMPROVEMENT! With that said, let me introduce myself to you properly.

I am going to take you back to the beginning; during the forging of the one they call X.

You will learn about three events that have helped to create the person I am today. You will learn about my support unit (my parents). I call that the beginning. You will also learn about the accident and the attack. With that said, let us start at...

The Beginning:

This starts just like any other story I suppose. I was born in the seventies in San Jose, California, back in 1971. My parents where the type of people who decided to have me at an early age, and I assumed it was because they wanted to be young enough to support me in all my young endeavors and just be there for me and do things like the normal American family would do! You know the kind of parents that you probably had growing up. Always there to keep you on track in school, get you ready for the next step in your life (college) and tell you about the birds and the bees when the time was right! The kind of parents to instill discipline when needed, and went to all your activities as a child and made you believe that you could take on the world and come out on top.

Does that sound familiar to you? Well I would not know anything about that, as that was not my life.

Now don't get me wrong here, I was blessed because for one, my mother had me at nineteen or 20 I think and at that age, I am sure the idea of abortion entered her thought process, and obviously she made the right choice because I am still here! I have no doubt that my parents loved me and I am grateful to both of them for doing the best they could (I think) for me while they were able to! However, it's time for me to share my point of view as to how it all went down for me!

As you can probably imagine, having a kid when you are still a kid, there is a great potential to be caught up with distractions. You know, those "certain things" in life that can keep one from focusing on the major task of raising a child! So those "certain things" for my parents came in the form of drugs. You see, I come from a very talented and musically inclined group of people who all have a talent for something. Not to mention we are all rather athletic too. My father was a keyboard player and to put it lightly, the man is good! He played for bands like Ike and Tina Turner back when they were together, Gladys Knight and the Pips, Bill Withers, The Gap Band, and a few others that I have forgotten about. Now when I say the man is good, I mean he is the type of guy who does not read music, but after listening to something, he could reproduce it, add his own style, and make it sound even better! Yeah he is that good.

Now with that kind of talent and that kind of exposure to the world, who would have time to deal with a child? Now as I recall, I came into the picture when his musical career was a bit slow. I remember being in my grandparent's living room and seeing pictures of my dad all dressed up in this white and gold studded outfit and this huge afro, back when he was a member of Ike's band. There were vinyl albums around the home which he recorded and signed,

I am thinking I have a really cool dad. I mean this is stuff I could take to show and tell right!

Well needless to say, with that kind of environment, the next natural progression would be to fall into the women, drugs, and more women, and my father, in true Smith fashion, did exactly that. By the time I was old enough to understand a few things going on around me, I realized his career as a famous musical genius was all but over. My parents were divorced before I was born and I spent the majority of my time being raised by my grandparents (God knew what he was doing).

Then there was my mother! Like I said, she did do what she could for me when she was in my life and I am thankful to her for that, but she, being younger than my father, sort of followed in his footsteps with the drugs and all. She also came from a strictly religious background and I suppose once she got a chance to experience the world and all it had to offer, she was going to be all in. After all it was my father that she said she really truly loved. Anyway, with two young people in love or should I say in lust, with a kid on the way, something had to give. Unfortunately my father gave in to the temptation of drugs, women, and the lifestyle of the rock star, and my mother just followed along.

As a result, I did not grow up with the typical environment of the loving parents, a pet, and the white picket fence. I did not have the support of parents who had gone to college and started a career the typical American way. There is NOTHING about me or my life that I consider average, normal or typical. And it is for this reason; I know I am here for a purpose. Now before we transition into another part of my life, I want to share this with you!

For as long as I can remember, I used to carry a big weight of resentment, anger, and bitterness around and it manifested in my relationships with others.

Now-a-days, you can hardly catch me without my patented smile and matching attitude toward life, but it was not always that way. You see, while I was primarily raised by my grandparents, there was the obvious generation gap that existed that in my opinion, can only be bridged by parents. So for the longest, I would look at other families with a bit of envy because they had supporting parents. People that cared about what they did and the people they hung out with. People who would encourage them to participate in sports or play some musical instrument! I am here to tell you that even at 6'2" and 252 lbs with body fat under 22%, not even I am strong enough to carry around that weight of bad energy. I have learned that doing such stupid acts as that only affected me. Instead of keeping that bad energy, I embrace all that has happened to me, I used it to forgive, and move on with my life! Now it's better for all parties involved! Okay so enough about the beginning. Now let's move on to...

The Accident:

The timeline for this incident was my sophomore year of high school. This was the time in my life when I was supposed to be getting comfortable with who I am, and what I am to contribute to the world. For me, I was more concerned with how I looked on my new moped with my Jerry curl, and more importantly I was concerned with how I was going to impress the new girl that lived across the street from my grandparents place.

No really, as a sophomore in high school with a moped, I thought I was on top of the world! You see, we lived with just enough. We did not have all the best of things, but we did not want for many things either. Kind of middle of the road with money I suppose. But I went to high school way out of my district at a school called Piedmont Hills. In my eyes, this was THE school to be in. We were dominant in basketball, really good in football, and everyone wanted to beat us and I got to be a part of that process. But anyway, this is about the accident.

So there I was, feeling high on life riding my moped, and wondering if life could get any better than this. There was a young girl who moved into the hood I wanted to impress her with my charm and wheels. Who could turn down a guy on a bike? So what it was a moped. It looked like a motorcycle okay. Give me a break. I had been pretending to have problems with my bike so I had to take it for a spin to make sure it was fixed. I was trying to come up with the courage to ask her if she wanted to ride. Lucky for her, we never made that far.

As I was pulling into the driveway, and giving the young lady a wink, it happened. According to the young lady and others who saw it, I was struck by a drunk driver in a yellow VW bug traveling at a high rate of speed in a residential neighborhood. They say I slid from the point of contact all the way over to the corner of my neighbor's home. That was over 50 feet. Get this, I had no protective equipment. No Helmet, no gloves, nothing! The result, I had a broken collar bone, a deep four inch shoulder laceration and a blood clot in my head that was the size of another head.

When I came to, I was already in the hospital with my grandparents overlooking and praying for me. My mother showed up some time later and my father never did show up. But I digress. When I tried to sit up, is when I learned about the blood clot. It was so heavy, that it kept me from sitting up! My outlook was bleak. I was in the hospital for two weeks. Now the point of my sharing this is to speak about purpose. Earlier I mentioned that one's life is shaped by events. Well this event, as traumatic as it was, happened for a reason, a purpose. I believe that nothing happens by accident! Are you starting to understand the true meaning of why I am happy to be alive? Listen, I am here to let you know that if you have breath within, YOU are here for a purpose! This event happened to me and something bigger than me saw fit for me to stick around for a while. Perhaps to share my story! If I can convince you of anything, I hope to convince you to live your purpose... whatever that may be. Now let's move on to...

The Attack:

So here is the scenario. I was 29 at the time, in the military stationed in Italy living in a beautiful city in Aviano, Italy. I had been working 12 hour shifts for months and a planned vacation was about to become a reality! The plan was to see my younger brother and his family in Arizona and boy was I excited to get there! You see, my brother, whom I regard as a big inspiration and a huge reason as to why I settled here in Arizona, is the person who got my entrepreneurial fire started.

He got here as a result of being a beast on the football field. His talents earned him a scholarship at Arizona State where he made a name for himself as a tenacious linebacker. Now taking his energy from the football field to the business of real estate, he also made a name for himself in the game of real estate as well. That's a whole other story in itself, but I digress. Let's get back to the attack.

So here I am, on leave from my military duty in Italy, being groomed to help out my brother in the real estate game. Seeking a break from learning the ropes of the the real estate game, we decided to play some basketball at ASU. Now keep in mind, that we were both physically active and keep in shape even to this day. But I am here to tell you straight up, you cannot out train a bad diet.

I remember it like it was yesterday, although it was actually over 10 years ago now. It happened on a Friday. We got into some serious pick- up games at the open gym floor of ASU's practice facility. Now I never really had jumping skills, unlike my brother who could jump out of the gym. But at 29, watching some of the youngsters fly off the court, made me happy to be retired, and just there to burn some calories, not to compete with these young bucks.

So after about two games I noticed tightness in my chest. So I am thinking it was just because I just ate right before heading out for the gym. So I kept playing. Midway through the third game, the feeling had progressed into feeling like an elephant had walked into the gym, sought me out, and sat on my chest! I mean the pain was so great, I had to pull myself out of the game! Once I did that, the pain subsided a bit and as a result I thought I had a severe case of gas or heartburn or something like that. So what do I do? Nothing. I ended up disregarding it and going home like nothing happened. Saturday rolls around and the pain which was at level 10 (the worst) the day before was now at about a 4 or five. So being the typical macho male who was still in shape, I thought the gas or heartburn was a thing of the past. Little did I know that I was wrong!

Saturday was uneventful as we just hung out and did the family thing, so there was really no physical activity to speak of that day, but the time bomb was ticking down to the event. I went to bed without incident, but upon waking up, the elephant had found me again and took up residence on my chest again. The funny thing is, this time if felt like that elephant had gained some weight! By now, I am in enough pain to warrant going to the hospital, so that's what we did! I am thinking, the doc was going to give me something for heartburn or gas and send me on my way, but that did not happen.

After some test had been run, and after they hooked me up to all these electrodes, the doctor comes back with a chart in his hand and tells me I had a myocardial infarction. Yes, I, at 29 years young, someone who was physically fit (so I thought) had a heart attack! Fortunately or unfortunately, depending on how you look at it, I was having this heart attack for 2 days! This attack left me in the hospital for two weeks. My artery was clogged by 50% with cholesterol. I now have a stint in my heart and I am supposed to be taking a bunch of medication for the rest of my life but that is another story! If you were to look at me today, you would not be able to tell I had a heart attack. You would not be able to tell I was hit by a drunk driver and left for dead. You would not be able to tell I was born to parents who just did not care about me as much as they cared about themselves!

You are not able to tell these things about me because I have chosen a path of excellence. This path requires forgiveness, and a desire to live by certain energy level, one that involves one of peace, tranquility, and Zen.

So you may ask why I am sharing all this with you. Well, it goes back to what I opened this with. It's all about purpose my friend! Life is pretty simple if you ask me. You can be a victim about the things that happen to you and go through life blaming others, and depending on others to make your life right. Or you can be a victor of your life and use your circumstances (the ones you can control, and the ones you can't) to empower yourself to a better life!

Look, everything happens for a reason, so you can either sit on the sideline and watch life go by or you can take some personal responsibility, start making a positive IMPACT, seek ways to INSPIRE yourself then others, keep IMPROVING, and like my main man Mark would suggest, get off the bench, and put into life what you want to get out of life!

I know there are many stories like this one, and perhaps you found some similarities in your own life, and if that is the case, may you find this story helpful to you or someone you know. After all, "It's Not About Me - It's About The Purpose Of Me!" I am Xavier Smith, aka, Mr. XL Smith and I thank you for reading!

This is My Story-For His Glory!!!

Xavier Smith

Rather than make the choice to be an eternal victim of life, Xavier now uses his life, the good, bad, and the ugly to be of service to others, by taking his God given talents and combining them with his passion for helping others get off the fence of mediocrity and start living life the way they see it in their mind!

Despite both parent being absent, surviving a hit-and-run accident, and a heart attack, Xavier is fully connected to his purpose of "Living The Mission!"

"I rely on my faith, family support and key people in my life to help me stay focused on the mission of serving others, because after all... it's not about me - it's about the purpose of me!"

@mrXLSmith
www.mrxlsmith.com
xs@mrxlsmith.com

My Vision, My Plan, MY NOW

Frustrated

Tieast Leverett

> *Here I sit*
> *With my shoes mismated.*
> *Lawdy-mercy!*
> *I's frustrated!*
>
> Langston Hughes, *Bad Morning*

You probably aren't expecting to read a chapter in this book from someone who is currently in a rut. My Vision, My Plan, My NOW is a compilation of motivational thoughts from some of the most driven people you can find; people who take ideas and bring them to fruition, people who put in the time and effort to become leaders in their chosen path, people who stop at nothing to reach the goals they have set for themselves…all of the contributors you have encountered in this book truly define success.

And then there's me.

Let me start off by giving you a glimpse of some of the things that have colored my past, the things that I used to define me.

I went to college with the sole intent of becoming a doctor. Not just any doctor, however. I wanted to do research on tropical diseases, because I was interested in helping people in developing countries. I was going to cure malaria once and for all... or something like that.

Long story short, I got off to a pretty good start, but problems soon set in. I quickly realized how easily I could be distracted, and what began as a promising academic life soon led to an impulsive transfer to a different university, academic suspension, some, shall we say..."legal" issues and an ultimate dropping out. I later hopped from school to school (again), had a few jobs, traveled quite a bit, finally got my degree, got married, had two kids, got divorced, moved halfway across the country and I am currently living my life in, you guessed it, my "rut".

The reason why I decided to write this chapter at this point in my life is because I know that for all the successes the other contributors in this book have had, they too (as I have and as you will) have experienced challenges and difficulties from which they thought they might never emerge.

If you asked any one of them, they would tell you that it was at that point; the moment they questioned themselves and their ability to succeed, that whatever decisions they made dictated the rest of their lives.

The thoughts you have at your lowest point are the ones that determine your path.

Here is what I have been thinking lately, and I'll let you know right up front that I left out a few things in that "story" about my life...but we will get to that soon.

When you're in a rut, you aren't as active as you may usually be, so first off, know that you will have an overabundance of time to think. Because of this, it is important to be very choosy about what you are thinking. My attention span can be pretty short, so I decided to use this time to challenge myself.

My challenge?

Sum up my life and the lessons within into brief statements that I could use to get myself back on path, simple thoughts that I could use to focus on positive things. Let's make it easy and call them the "Rut Rules". If you find yourself where I am, you might want to make your own list, but here are a few of mine that you can use.

Rut Rule #1: Don't waste time not being "you"

I know you've heard this in some form time and time again...because it's the truth. Are any of these familiar?

"One can have no smaller or greater mastery than mastery of oneself" - Leonardo da Vinci

*"This above all: **to thine own self be true**, and it must follow, as the night of the day, thou canst not then be false to any man"* - William Shakespeare

"Know Thyself" - Socrates

One of the most important things about getting to your vision, your plan and ultimately your NOW is knowing who YOU truly are.

Everyone says it, but most don't *really* do it. In my rut I am discovering more things about myself all the time; some of the things have been great. Others, I probably really didn't care to know, but THOSE are the things I need to fix.

You too should go through this process in whatever way you choose to get the most honest, most insightful and "realest" answers. You may not like what you find in there, but that's the starting point for change.

If you think you know yourself already, that's great! ...and also very naive.

You and I both know that people change and evolve constantly, so try to reevaluate yourself from time to time. You may be surprised at what you find.

Rut Rule #2: Listen closely to those who know you

One of the easiest ways to learn who you are is by really listening to those who KNOW you. I have a real problem with this.

Not that I don't want to hear it, but I usually think people don't have a clue what they are taking about when it comes to me, so it sounds like chatter going in one ear and out of the other.

My mistake.

A long time ago, my father said to me, "You have the characteristics of a journalist. You really should look at being a writer". Now, even though I had won several writing contests, had received accolade after accolade about my writing, loved writing so much that I did it just for fun and had received writing assignments from newspapers and magazines with no formal training, I disregarded his wisdom, because as you know, I was going to cure malaria...or something like that.

After several forays into several different careers I've now found that yes; I am probably going to end up as a journalist.

This is also the same person who said (as he walked me down the aisle to my anxiously awaiting soon-to-be-ex-husband), "Are you sure you want to do this? We don't have to." This (after he had paid an obscene amount of money for this wedding) was absurd to me. Of course I wanted to do this! The story of how that turned out is for another book at another other time, but trust me...THAT would be a great read.

My father knew better that I did at the time who I was inside, what drove me, what my strengths were and who I was as a person...unfortunately for me I tuned out his words on these and many more occasions.

Again, ask the people that *really* know you; I'm not talking about the fly-by-night friend, or the overly analytical family member or your friendly co-worker...I mean the people who have observed you CLOSELY for years. The people who love you unconditionally and have your best interest at heart are the only ones you need to reach out to for this. Ask them what they see as your strengths, what they see as your weaknesses and how they view you as a person holistically.

Then take what they say and use it. I know I will this time.

Rut Rule #3: Pull the trigger, but expect the recoil

The first weapon I ever fired was a Luger. Keeping in mind I'm about 5'3" and at the time was just around 120lbs.

Needless to say, I generated raucous laughter from the rest of the people (even more so from my cop friend) who stood next to me at the firing range where I was learning how to shoot.

I think my face alone had everyone in fits of hysteria, but I couldn't help it...I was completely unprepared for the recoil. I didn't fall over, but I was close to it.

The same seems to have gone for my life. There have been many times that I have not been prepared for the consequences of my actions, and in several instances, I have "fallen over" because of them.

Maybe you've experienced this as well, but as you look toward your NOW, you must remember that once you make a decision (and take action) there will always be a result. Furthermore, it really makes no difference whether the result is good or bad...in either case, you must be prepared for the recoil.

If you remember, in my "story" I mentioned that I had transferred universities, and that my decision to do so was impulsive.

It definitely was.

Believe me...there was little planning or research on my part before I "pulled the trigger", or in other words, took action and transferred. The "recoil", or results of my actions were extremely negative. I went from being on the Dean's List to struggling to even make it to class. I was definitely not ready for that scenario.

But, despite suffering extreme academic setback, this decision had another consequence. Through an unusual chain of events, it afforded me the opportunity to study abroad in West Africa. Other than parenting, this was the single most life-altering experience I've ever had. So looking at it another way, the result was positive. I can't say I was completely ready for it at the time, but I have definitely grown immensely from it.

Your perspective on the results of your actions is key... especially when you're looking at them from a rut.

Rut Rule #4: Sometimes all you need IS the clothes on your back

I am an expert at making excuses...hence my current status. (This is an example of one of the things I learned during Rut Rule #1).

Many of you may be good at this too, or know other "experts" in the field, and unfortunately it is an easy field to enter.

As for me, I haven't pursued that new idea or taken steps toward a goal or made that call to a possible mentor or developed that business proposal and sent it or taken that trip or gone to that meeting or read that book or emailed that article or...

You get the idea.

The reasons why I haven't done any of these things are just as numerous. I am way too busy with kids, or I'm too tired, I deserve a break, I don't have any ideas, my computer isn't charged, I have to go to the store, I want to watch the Bears on Monday night, (or the Bulls or the Sox...can you guess where I grew up?), I don't know enough about the subject to write, I don't have a business degree, journalism degree or I am not finished with my master's degree so I can't, and blah, blah, blah...

My excuses are endless. Well, not exactly...they end in a rut.

So from down here, I decided once again to change my thinking. I decided to think of times when I started with nothing and made something happen out of it.

Think back to my "story". I moved from Chicago to Philadelphia a few years ago, when my marriage was over. Here is what I had with me as I drove halfway across the country:

1. Car
2. Two Kids
3. Clothes on our backs (and a few toys to keep them quiet)

I completely started over; with no choice but to dive right in. I had a new job, in a new city, a new status as a single mom, a new house, a new school for my kids...everything was a new experience.

Within six months, I was responsible for clients within a territory comprised of the entire southeastern half of the country (no prior sales experience), I was actively involved in community organizations and my son had been designated as gifted in three subjects.

In another eight months, I had a job offer for a Department of Defense contract training position in IT (no prior IT experience either), and I packed my kids up once again and moved a few hours south down to the DC area. Again, new house, new job, new school, new, new, new...

Within a year of that move, I was once again in community organizations (this time holding an office), vice-president of my kids PTA, the recipient of accolades on my job, the developer of a training program that I implemented in Accra, Ghana (as a side project of my own interest), and a published writer for a few online outlets. By the way...my kids are still spectacular students.

That's quite a far cry from the person who unflinchingly drove across Illinois, Indiana, Ohio and Pennsylvania into the unknown... with nothing but the clothes on her back.

I may be in a rut right now, but the more I focus on "her"; that person that you just read about in the last few paragraphs, I am more convinced that the days of this rut are numbered. As soon as I can get "her" back, all of the excuses I am making will be meaningless. *I had everything I needed in that car to be a success; me and the ones who loved me the most.*

As for you, I don't know who you are, what you may be going through or where you are in the process of claiming your NOW. But I do know one thing...all you need to claim your NOW is this:

1. YOU
2. The ones who love and support you
3. The clothes on your back

Find a way...or make one... with the tools you already have.

Rut Rule #5: Do something for someone, just because

There is a Caribbean saying that goes loosely like this, "Always treat others with the utmost kindness...you never know when they will need to return the favor".

While I don't necessarily disagree with this quote, I don't fully agree with it either. I think people should do things for others with no expectation of something in return.

I especially think this is important when you are in a rut. In fact, nothing has helped me more during these past few months. I spend a considerable amount of my time volunteering at my children's school, and in several community organizations, but the ones I like the best are opportunities with children and women in underserved communities.

Maybe you prefer helping with animals, reading to the elderly, volunteering with veterans or faith-based opportunities...doesn't matter, find something that compels you to act.

And go act.

Sometimes a talk with a WWII Veteran can help bring clarity to your VISION. Sometimes rescuing a malnourished dog can help you find the missing piece or person to help solidify your PLAN. Sometimes helping a teen mother can enrich your NOW in a powerful way, and can give you more passion and drive to continue toward your success.

Now that I think about it, maybe the Caribbean saying was right. You really never know when your kindness may be returned...or what it is you might receive.

Well I'll end this here, but I've got a few more Rut Rules in mind. If you're interested, you can always email me at any time.

And I hope, should you ever find yourself where I am, that something here can help you...but hurry up, because I won't be down here in this rut much longer.

TIEAST LEVERETT

Tieast Leverett is a corporate trainer and freelance writer with global clientele, who is extremely passionate about serving the community. She has worked as a motivational speaker for Making it Count Programs, as a Corporate Narrator for Mazda North American Operations, as a crew member for United Airlines, has been published in over 20 publications, and she has served as a trainer for the US Army and several other private entities in the US and West Africa.

She attended Hampton University, University of Ghana-Legon, and received her Bachelor's Degree in Biological Sciences from DePaul University. She is currently working on a Master's in International Diplomacy and is building hours toward earning a private pilot's license. She is an avid traveler, a gourmet chef and enjoys reading, foreign languages and sharing her experiences with her two children.

"There is nothing like returning to a place that remains unchanged to find the ways in which you yourself have altered." - Nelson Mandela

Email: **tieastleverett@gmail.com**

My Vision, My Plan, MY NOW

Part 3: MY NOW

My Vision, My Plan, MY NOW

What NOW? Using Life's Pitfalls to Fall Forward

Torski Dobson-Arnold

The 7 Key Characteristics of Resiliency in Success

Life can certainly deal us a tough hand at times, can't it? First, the car breaks down and there's an unexpected bill we hadn't planned for. A few days later, one of the kids brings home a note that requests your presence at an impromptu parent/teacher conference. And just when things couldn't get any more congested, the boss comes in to a staff meeting and announces a new project that needs to be completed by the end of the quarter. Ooh, and by the way, he wants you to head up the project that includes 2 other department associates. Yes, life can become very overwhelming at times causing many of us to throw our hands up in the air with a, "I'm done; I give up!" gesture. Life happens to all of us; however, some of us seem to be able to navigate the roadblocks, pitfalls, and sometimes downright "bad luck" that plagues each of us, better than others. So, what gives? How is it that some manage negative setbacks like a pro and others fall flat?

Successful people, those that are able to "fall forward" despite obvious mishaps and unfortunate events are those that possess 5 key characteristics and immerse these characteristics into their lives naturally.

These five characteristics are as follows:

1. Unwavering Positive Attitude
2. Action Plan in Motion (Plan Bs & Plan Cs)
3. Visualization of Success
4. Service Mindset
5. Gratitude of N.O.W.

Unwavering Positive Attitude

The main ingredient of the successful person's psyche that allows them to move forward regardless of life's pitfalls is their unwavering positive attitude. Successful people develop this commitment to always seeing the glass half full versus half empty. How you may ask? Basically, those that commit themselves to being successful both professionally and personally adopt the philosophy that they control their own destiny. "If it is meant to be, it's up to me" is almost always the battle cry from these types of individuals. This is adopted through continuous and gradual positive reinforcements to include positive affirmations and daily positive self-talk. Over time, like any habit, this ideology becomes the natural and normal understanding. With this new unwavering spirit, it takes more than a flat tire or a rude fast food worker to push successful people off of their "center."

How can we build up our attitude to be more positive than negative? Expect the best. If you go through life, looking for the best in others, events, and opportunities, then you will be able to find the best in all things, even the obvious setbacks in life. Somebody once said, "You will always find what you look for" and they were so right. I'm sure you know someone that always speaks negative about EVERYTHING.

Life is never good. The weather is never nice. He/she can ALWAYS find the worst in another person. Their perspective is their truth, but if you, in contrast, seek out and look hard to find the best in EVERYTHING, then you will live out your own truth. This mindset, over time, will draw "like to like" and everything, even the bumps in the road called life, will work out for your good.

Questions/Tips to move you past the "What Now?"

- What is one thing I can I do to create a positive outlook for my life?
- How might this attitude benefit those around me at home and at work?

Action Plan in Motion (Plan Bs & Plan Cs)

Do you know someone, a close friend, maybe even a family member that can ALWAYS give you an excuse as to why they didn't do this, or finish that, or start yet? Think of the last time someone had this type of conversation with you. Now recall more of the conversation, if you can, as to what reason that person used for not accomplishing that task or goal? Why didn't they complete that degree? Why didn't they get started on that dream?

Was the reason a valid one or did they offer a mere excuse for not pushing through, around, over or under the obstacle? Did they take any personal responsibility for not getting it done?

Successful people create actions plans for goals and dreams in life. Successful people create daily, monthly, and annual action items with due dates to move them closer to accomplishing their goals.

Like me, at times, even the most successful person realizes that they need a kick in the butt to stay on task. Successful people will build support systems like accountability partners and join mastermind groups to hold themselves accountable for making sure that they are moving along with the pursuit of goals in a timely, relevant, and strategic manner.

Successful people use step-by-step action plans as motivation to build momentum and guide their actions and mindset to stay laser focused and not become distracted. If you are looking for a reason to stop, give up, or put your dreams on hold, you don't have to look very far. Accomplishing goals in pursuit of our dreams can be a daunting endeavor and because of this, life can and will easily provide every "woulda, coulda, shoulda" excuse in the book to use to give up. I want to challenge you to create Plan A, B & C so that when a roadblock occurs you can easily chart a new course on your professional goals GPS, and move right around that issue and keep pressing forward.

Questions/Tips to move you past the "What Now?"

- Identify a Plan A goal that didn't work out for me last time. What's the next step, my Plan B? What can I do differently to make this plan work?

- What roadblocks might I encounter in this plan? How am I going to plan for them instead of letting them "happen" to me?

Visualization of Success

During an interview at the height of his illustrious professional career, a reporter asked Michael Jordan how he was able to claim victory in a playoff game or in a championship game and then deliver on his prediction. MJ shared that because of his unwavering belief in himself and that of his Chicago Bulls teammates, he had already seen the success of his team, he had already seen himself taking the winning shot at the buzzer, and that he knew this with a steadfast certainty because he had long visualized holding the championship trophy. He knew what being a winner felt like and what success already looked like. When it came to playing the actual game, all he was doing was replaying what he had already seen in his mind's eye.

Visualization is a very powerful tool used by successful people to create the outcomes they seek in their personal and professional lives. When the highs and lows of life draw a different picture for the successful person, they take this new snapshot all in stride knowing that the vision they've seen is just around the corner. They live in the philosophy that everything has purpose and that a downfall is a learning opportunity to grow and recommit to the dream and/or goal.

Many people practice just the opposite for their lives. Instead they replay over and over again the bad situations that have played out in their lives, reliving the emotions and stress involved in managing these negative situations. We have to make the decision and commitment to dwell on and visualize the positives versus the negatives which can easily be infused into our lives through repetition.

> *Questions/Tips to move you past the "What Now?"*

- Close your eyes and think about finally accomplishing that big dream you've had for a long time. How did you do it?
- Who is celebrating my accomplishment with me? Where am I celebrating my accomplishment?
- When is the dream accomplished? (How old am I?)
- Who has supported me in my journey of this accomplishment?

Tap into all areas of your psyche to make visualization a part of your everyday life. Write out what being successful in your professional life will look like. Speak out loud to yourself first thing in the morning and before you go to sleep at night on the details of your success. Use vivid language and imagery to create the image of success in your heart and mind.

Service Mindset

Successful people, through their actions, remind us through powerful demonstrations of motivation how to stay on our path of success – by serving others. Successful people live another very important theory in their lives.

"To whom much is given, much is required."

Through strategic planning, visualization, and a positive attitude, successful people had made major strides in accomplishing their goals and aspirations in life. Because of this level of success, it is important and absolutely vital to serve others. On the surface, it may appear that by serving others you give more of yourself and get back less in return, but nothing could be more from the truth.

Serving others allows individuals to share and touch a life in a meaningful and impactful way. By serving, successful people challenge themselves and their thinking, apply strategic planning tools to solve problems for others, and connect with new and diverse populations stretching their norm and creating new meaningful relationships.

By cultivating this service mindset, the successful person has the opportunity to "shake up" the status quo and humble him/her to focus on the pulse of the people and the world.

Those that falter under the first sign of distress in life focus on just the opposite and subscribe to another channel – the "WIFM: What's in it for me station?" This strains empathy and opportunity for the dismayed and disenchanted individual that can't seem to understand why life is so hard to them and how they can never change their current situation. Creating a service mindset continuously feeds the cups of hope and determination.

Questions/Tips to move you past the "What Now?"

- What are some areas in my neighborhood or at work where I can use my gifts and talents to serve others?
- Is there someone that I know that I can reach out and help with a personal or professional pursuit?

Gratitude of N.O.W.

Ever met an individual that always identified a future date or event as the catalyst to their happiness? "When I get a new job, I'll be satisfied." "Once I find a mate and get married, then I'll be happy." "I will be set, if I win the lottery."

This is a falsehood perpetuated by a commercialized society that has trained us to think that we need more of this, less of this, this person, that person, or this particular situation to happen to truly have happiness in our lives. Let me ask you a question, "What's right, right now?" Seriously, there'll always be something else we want, think we need, or wish for, but our happiness can never be measured based on these superficial things. If you think you need that new car to be happy, just talk with the man or woman who has no car and has to walk to work, walk their kids to school, walk to the local market to make groceries and catch the bus to the hospital for a serious medical situation. Getting that new car doesn't seem all that important anymore, does it? Particularly if your current car is in working order and pretty good shape.

Or let's talk to the single parent that lost their mate during their deployment overseas and now has to raise their 3 kids alone, trying to work through their own grief and hold it all together emotionally and financially for the kids' sake. Let's re-evaluate minimizing our happiness because we haven't met the right person to marry yet. Are we not currently grateful for the beautiful, smart, savvy, witty, and energetic YOU that you are right now? Why are you not happy "enough" in the fact that you are in your right mind, given a reasonable portion of health, and woke up to see a brand new day with the understanding that there are thousands just like you all across this world that didn't get the chance you've been given?

Being grateful in the N.O.W. stands for NEVER OVERLOOKING WINS in your life. Every day presents us with new wins that we should take the time to be appreciative of. Our family, our friends, our jobs and professions (despite the fact that you may be looking for new opportunities), our health, and our unwavering dreams and aspirations all represent a sampling of wins that we have already accomplished.

It is true that successful people unapologetically strive for new heights and new goals pushing themselves outside of their comfort zone, but rest assured that this passion and drive does not eradicate the fact that they recognize and show gratitude for the "what's right" in their lives. This is a huge part of building up the resiliency necessary for tomorrow's successes. If we spend too much attention on what's coming into our lives in the future and completely ignore the N.O.W., then the areas of our lives that currently work for our good will crumble given the lack of attention and care shown to it.

Many times when life starts to take some bumpy turns and twist, we can easily get caught up in those situations and forget the gratitude that needs to be shown in the N.O.W. I want to challenge you to stay humbled and focus on what's right in your life to keep you grounded and moving forward to your success.

Questions/Tips to move you past the "What Now?"

- Can I identify the N.O.W.s in my life?
- How have I been treating them?

- Have I been appreciating and being grateful for what's right in my world?

Every day I will identify times when I might take my wins for granted and immediately transition that thought to one of gratefulness instead.

Successful people, those that are able to "fall forward" despite obvious mishaps and unfortunate events are those that possess 5 key characteristics and immerse these characteristics into their lives naturally. Those five characteristics are (1) Unwavering Positive Attitude, (2) Action Plan in Motion (Plan Bs & Plan Cs), (3) Visualization of Success, (4) Service Mindset, and (5) Gratitude of N.O.W.

Nobody's perfect and even the most successful people don't get it right all the time. If you have been battling setbacks and mishaps in life for all too long that have caused your dreams to be put on hold and on the sidelines, I am here to tell you that TODAY is the DAY. So, "What Now?" Now you've got a new way of managing your thoughts, which in turn will alter your actions and ultimately transition your outcomes to WINS not just for the short-term, but for your life. Don't wait, pick just one characteristic to hone in on first and then gradually add one more and so on and so forth. Rome wasn't built in a day and neither do your dreams have to be. We're all going to fall sometimes, my charge for you, Fall Forward, Get Up and Do Something Different NOW.

TORSKI DOBSON-ARNOLD

Torski Dobson-Arnold, PHR is America's Top Career Confidence Coach & Chief Career Strategist of Your Career Confidence, LLC, a career services firm dedicated working with job seekers to get noticed and get hired quicker. As a professional motivator, Torski has spoken to over 50,000 participants with national programs such as Rachel's Challenge and Monster's Making it Count programs.

To book Torski for your next speaking event or keynote address, please visit www.torskidobsonarnold.com.

To hire a qualified career strategist to work with you to get noticed by employers and get hired today, please visit **www.yourcareerconfidence.com.**

Torski can also be reached at **torski@yourcareerconfidence.com** or **804-921-8180.**

My Vision, My Plan, MY NOW

Redefining an Image
Jonathan Oliver

Since 2001, DNA testing has freed 12 men in Dallas County, Texas. The latest example of new DNA tests overturning old convictions came this past January. In the case, 50-year-old James Waller was convicted of raping a 12-year-old boy in 1982, a crime he said he never committed. When asked how he felt about being wrongly convicted, Mr. Waller, said "I have no hatred towards anyone, because I have made my peace with God."

We are constantly going through a metamorphosis and there will come a time in life where we must redefine our image. Hopefully it will not be at the magnitude of James Waller's experience. No matter what the situation is, I believe that there are three key factors in redefining an image: forgiveness, a positive attitude, and good deeds.

Forgiveness

Susan St. James said, "Having resentment is like taking poison and hoping the other person dies." Forgiveness is the first key factor in redefining an image. Forgive the people that hurt you. Forgive that boss that did you wrong. Forgive that friend who betrayed you. Forgive that parent that mistreated you when you were younger. Get rid of all that poison. Don't let that root of bitterness grow deeper and continue to contaminate your life. What does this toxic waste look like in your life? For some people it seeps out as anger. In others it looks like depression. For others it reeks of low self-esteem. You are not forgiving the people that hurt you for their sake, but for your sake. You are forgiving in order not to carry that baggage around. The hardest forgiveness I had to show towards someone was…I. I could forgive others, I could pray to God and ask Him to forgive me, however I couldn't forgive myself. Did I hold myself at a higher level than God? Did I expect more from my life than God, then why couldn't I forgive myself. So on December 12, 2006, I sat down at my dinner table and I wrote a letter to myself. I addressed it "Dear Jonathan Oliver." In the letter I expressed all of my 'could haves', 'would haves', and 'should haves'. I expressed my regrets and remorse. I wrote from my heart and I let it all out. After I finished writing the letter, I read it out loud. Then I typed it out, signed it and dated it. Finally I put it in a frame and placed it on top of my bookcase beside my college degree. Now, having truly felt the freedom of self forgiveness, when I feel that I am being too hard on myself or that there is no way my situation could improve, I read that letter addressed "Dear Jonathan Oliver."

Positive Attitude

Buddha said, "Holding on to anger is like grasping a hot coal with the intent of throwing it at someone else; you are the one getting burned." Having a positive attitude is the next factor in redefining an image. Evaluate where you are. Ask yourself what brought you to this point. Are you learning or are you merely doing the same thing over and over again? Doing the same thing over and over while expecting to get different results is the definition of insanity. Stop and change your approach. Accept responsibility for your life--don't be a volunteer victim. Be determined to handle any challenge in a way that will make you grow. Take charge of your emotions. Learn to master them or they will master you. You see examples of this almost every day when you open the newspaper or turn on your TV. Someone is apologizing for letting their emotions get the best of them. Lastly, expect things to get better. An anonymous author wrote an inspiring poem about perseverance, simply titled "Don't Quit."

DON'T QUIT

When things go wrong as they sometimes will,

When the road you're trudging seems all uphill,

When the funds are low and the debts are high,

And you want to smile, but you have to sigh,

When care is pressing you down a bit,

Rest, if you must but don't you quit.

Life is queer with its twists and turns,

As every one of us sometimes learns.

And many a failure turns about,

When they might have won had they stuck it out:

Don't give up, though the pace seems slow

You may succeed with another blow.

Often the struggler has given up

When they might have captured the victor's cup

And they learned too late, when the height slipped down

How close they were to the golden crown

Success is failure turned inside out.

The silver tint of the clouds of doubt.

And you can never tell how close you are

It may be near when it seems afar.

So stick to the fight when you're hardest hit-

It's when things seem worst that you mustn't quit.

Remember what Charles Swindoll said: "Life is 10% what happens to us and 90% how we react to it." Have a positive attitude.

Good Deeds

Too much talk is just like chalk...you can rub it out. Napoleon Hill once said: "deeds, and not words are what count the most." Doing good deeds is the final factor in redefining an image. If you are spending a lot of time and energy feeling sorry for yourself, find someone you can help and forget about yourself for a while. Whenever I am having a self pity day, I call my great-grandmother. She turned 87 earlier this year and she is my "Big Mama." She enjoys a good conversation and she can talk for hours. Something special happens during the course of our conversation. As we begin to say our 'good byes' to one another, I almost always notice that whatever I was feeling down and out about wasn't as huge as I made it out to be. The next time you're having a self absorbed day, hold a door open a few extra seconds and let some people in and out of a building. Slow down and allow few cars to merge onto the freeway the next time you are in bumper to bumper traffic.

Three individuals who did not let trials and tribulations stop them from doing good deeds-were Moses, Gandhi, and Nelson Mandela. Moses killed an Egyptian who was beating a Hebrew slave. Fearing that he would have to answer to Pharaoh, Moses went into hiding for over forty years. Until God spoke to him through a burning bush and we all know how the story ends. God used Moses to lead the Israelites who had been in slavery for over 400 years out of Egypt.

Gandhi had been imprisoned for many years on numerous occasions in both South Africa and India for his beliefs and practices. Throughout his life, Gandhi remained committed to non-violence and truth, even in the most extreme situations, which eventually led India to independence and inspired movements through the world. In India he is recognized as the Father of the Nation. Time magazine named Gandhi the Man of the Year in 1930 and the runner-up to Albert Einstein as "Person of the Century" at the end of 1999. Gandhi never received the Nobel Peace Prize, though he was nominated five times between 1937and 1948.

My Vision, My Plan, MY NOW

Nelson Mandela was in prison for 27 years as a result of his struggle against apartheid. Apartheid, meaning separatism, was a system of racial segregation that was enforced in South Africa beginning in 1948, and was dismantled in 1993. Nelson Mandela was the first President of South Africa to be elected in fully representative democratic elections. In 1993 awarded, the Nobel Peace Prize for his work in terminating the apartheid regime, and for laying the foundations for a new democratic South Africa. According to Time 100, he is one of only four people in history to have helped shape both the 20th and 21st centuries. The other three are Bill Gates, Pope John II, and Oprah Winfrey.

Good were a key factor which allowed Moses, Gandhi, and Nelson Mandela to move forward and experience the true value of their lives after going through trials and tribulations. What you give is what you get.

Like James Waller, you are freeing yourself from bondage when you forgive the people who hurt you. Have a positive attitude, don't dwell on yesterday's disappointments or your past failures, press forward, and look for the goodness that is in store for you. When you are feeling sorry for yourself, do something nice for someone else. What you give is what you get. Marianne Williamson, in her book *A Return to Love*, wrote a passage that is often mistakenly attributed to Nelson Mandela as part of his inaugural address as President of South Africa.

Our deepest fear is not that we are inadequate.

Our deepest fear is that we are powerful beyond measure.

It is our Light, not our Darkness, that most frightens us.

We ask ourselves, who am I to be brilliant, gorgeous, talented, fabulous?

Actually, who are you NOT to be?

You are a child of God. Your playing small does not serve the World.

There is nothing enlightening about shrinking.

So that other people won't feel unsure around you.

We were born to manifest the glory of God that is within us.

It is not just in some of us; it is in everyone.

As we let our own light shine.

We unconsciously give other people permission to do the same.

As we are liberated from our own fear,

Our presence automatically liberates others.

No matter what the situation is, I believe forgiveness, a positive attitude, and good deeds are the key factors to redefining an image.

JONATHAN OLIVER

Jonathan believes that life is what we are born with; living is what we do with it. His mission is to create a world of truth, love, and faith by helping individuals to harness their gifts and talents. He earned a Bachelor of Behavioral Science in 2003 majoring in Psychology, with a minor in Biology. He is the founder of Higher Enlightenment which he started in 2005. Higher Enlightenment is a firm that provides spiritual and intelligent insight to others which helps them to believe in themselves and reach beyond their fears. By assisting them in this he assists others in living their dreams.

Jonathan is a dynamic speaker and has presented a variety of programs to over 6000,000 people. He is also the author of *Impersonations,* which was released in 2009. It is an inspirational book that shares how he overcame dyslexia and a recovery program to live his dream.

Jonathan is a certified speaker for Monster's Making It Count Programs, where he speaks to high school and college students throughout the country on preparing for college and career. He is also a certified speaker for Rachel's Challenge, an organization committed to inspire, equip, and empower every person to create a permanent positive culture of change in their schools, businesses, and communities by starting a chain reaction of kindness and compassion.

Omnipresence... Now
Nysheva-Starr

The water was warm, assisted by the sun marking it up. Her feet felt vindicated for a rejuvenating submersion as the salt purified them. The air blew, calmly, yet sternly, just enough to allow for the sand to rise up and meet her skin. She marveled at the sand racing up to meet her, reminiscing of the times THEN, when she raced to plow her hands down to meet *it*. She had been memorized by its infinitum since she was a kid, digging for hours *just* to meet the substance at the 'bottom' that she had encountered at the top. But, that didn't stop her from doing the exact same thing the next time she was at the beach. It was like, 'she had to dig.' Even when she knew she wouldn't discover anything so different, aside from a lone shell masked underneath that unearthed some temporary joy of purpose, she still dug. Digging, for her, was bigger than her, although she couldn't explain why. Numerous times, she stood flabbergasted when her parents harassed her with an explanation about her obsession. They justified her actions to family and friends, when "why is she always digging?" came up. "She's just being a toddler, all kids are curious" her mother would say. "But, its dirt," they'd say. By age three, she had replaced digging in sand as her favorite thing to do with digging in dirt, entranced by the unknown that awaited her. "She'll outgrow it," her father added, in a tone that would quickly change the subject. Yet, away from others, they would worry. She often heard them trying to speak in whispers, but failing just as the doctors had in reassuring them that nothing was wrong with her. It was harder for her mother who, 'just wanted their little girl to be okay.' "Maybe it *is* Asperger's," her mother said, "the constant engagement in one thing to an abnormal degree, we can get her tested again," she said to her mate, seeking confirmation. "There's nothing wrong with our daughter," he'd say, "she just does things differently," replied the father. "She Digs," for hours, her mother said, "like she's looking for something, like she's trying to discover something." "Maybe she is," her father would say and once again, end the conversation. She smiled, somewhat irresolutely as a wave hit her above her ankles to welcome her back. Her parents were stifled by her actions during those beginning years. And she couldn't help them. She didn't have an answer. How do you explain *seeing* something because you *feel* it so clearly? And, she wasn't stymied by 'being different,' instead impassioned by it.

Varied colored buckets covered the porch outside their home with labels in her five year old penmanship distinguishing the contents of one from the other. She created a new bucket each time she discovered a new organism. She separated the worms from the beetles from the ants from the spiders from the termites from the ticks from the flying organisms that she learnt to stop trying to catch. She even color coordinated supplies and notebooks she convinced her parents to buy for her so that she could more astutely care for each 'ecosystem.' She was treating all the different types of bugs and insects as if they were her pets. "They (were) her pets!" she'd answered defensively. And she was always fascinated by digging for more of them during her leisure. Her buckets grew as she grew and soon her parents bypassed her pastime as a part of herself.

By pre-adolescence, her 'insect/bug farm' was over three years old, but, her organism acumen seemed way beyond. And it wasn't because she was way smarter than other eight years old. It was because she was always doing things that 'normal' eight year olds didn't want to do or wasn't or wouldn't do. It wasn't that she was trying to stand alone; she just had stuff to do. She researched each organism's way of life and living in every field trip, museum, library and backyard. She journaled everything: observations, findings and questions and sought to answer each question in her notebook. She observed their movements under different natural conditions like excessive rain or sun and manmade imposed conditions, like clutter, accidental litter thrown in the buckets, and shifting the buckets too much or too hard. For some time, she had stopped adding families to the buckets as she watched the families grow. Besides, her parents were not going to allow her to get buckets any larger than the fourth time that she had changed them. But, she continued to dig. When her class was being introduced to evolution, she spat out that, "cockroaches was some of the oldest organisms to live," because they knew how to a-valve." She hadn't had fluidity with her new word yet. But, her ingenuity prompted her teacher to do a series of lessons on bugs and insects and she was thrilled to be able to allow her peers to partake in her knowledge even as she singlehandedly provided all the specimens for the discussions from her bucket collections. Her tenacity earned her school an improved science department and her awards in biology. Her parents beamed, probably elated that all her time with her 'friends' was leading to something, although they weren't sure what. But, the accolades from her peers who seemed to relinquish some of their thoughts of her being "weird" to her being "cool" and her parents who, after her continuous recognition, would sporadically peek in on her collection with some sort of abated interest while sparsely reminding her to take care of them if she seemed to be lacking in responsibilities, could not provide the solace that digging did.

Digging transcended for her, losing her to her thoughts for hours. Its hypnotic trance was a deliberate, induced meditation that liberated her. It became her haven, especially during times of emotional turmoil. "But, why, don't you just care for the bugs," her mom would say peevishly annoyed that 'the digging' was NOW futile since she wasn't adding any more organisms to the buckets. "Some of them are insects," she'd throw in snidely. "You know what I mean," her mother added, unimpressed. "Because it's a part of me," she said, imploring for understanding. 'Dirt is not a part of anyone," her mother would challenge. "Well, it's who I want to be, it's what I want to do. I know there are people who work -" "No one works *in* dirt," her mother harangued, interrupting her. "I want to work *with* dirt," she corrected, "because its like, the beginning and ending of almost everything." "There's always something new to expect even if there's nothing new *that* day," she continued. "It's where NOW is, it's what NOW is, it's how NOW is," she stopped dumfounded. That was the first time she had heard herself express herself with such clarity. Her mother almost froze, she had had bouts of witnessing the result of her daughter growing up, but, just NOW, she experienced the growing in the midst of the growth. They stood silent, looking at each other, but not looking, more like digging for compassion from the other. Her mother walked away in awe at the eleven year old who had dug her way through to an understanding of what she believed her purpose was.

She absently continued on *this* path, as if she was subconsciously confident that it was leading her somewhere. Most times, she was so vested in her 'caring for ritual' that she had to precariously remind herself of *other* things that were important and necessary to do. 'Remember to clean the bathroom and kitchen before going out to 'the farm' was inked on her hand when other teenagers were trying to see how many numbers they could accumulate on their arms,' she recalled with nostalgia. Teachers marveled blankly at the words like they were some cryptic hieroglyphics to help her cheat on test, but, her record of success and a confirmation from her parents quickly erased those thoughts. "You don't have to check on *them* NOW," her mom said annoyingly, "it can wait till LATER." "Yes," she replied, "but, why should it?" "You're always so much in a rush to check on those damn bugs," her mother jeered. "There's *also* insec-," she began. "And freaking insects," her mother added beratingly, before she got the rest of the word out, "you know what I mean child, stop playing with me," her mother finished admonishingly. "I'm not in a rush to check on them, I just don't know why I would wait until LATER to do something I feel an urge to do NOW. NOW is the only thing I feel NOW, so it is all I have to respond to...NOW," she said matter-of-factly as if she was delivering the logic as she was speaking it. "I think your mother just wants you to be *as* mindful with your chores and with spending time with your family as you are with other things that are important to you," her father said suggestively, his voice entering the space and parting the sedated tension between mother and daughter. "I'll do better," she said and smiled while walking away. "It's not working," she said to herself, during one of her 'spells,' as she spade away in a new area in the forest. "What's not working?" she had asked herself back. "I don't know," she responded, "but, I have to do things differently." That was her turning point.

From those days when being a teenager was enough of a challenge, she adopted a new approach to her living. She would approach her life like she did her 'farm.' She wrote notes for almost everything, including her daily routine until she memorized it and when it changed, she started the process over again. She color sequenced priorities, even making assessments of what strategies worked under which conditions and logging them in her new set of journals. Like, she learnt that if did an impromptu act for her parents, like made them a surprise breakfast or engaged her younger siblings for a full day to give them a break, her parents appeared beyond gracious. They'd offer her extra incentives: extra allowance, more mall time, 'farm duty' – 'the works.' Most of time, she'd decline, (except for with 'farm duty,' since she felt that nestling organisms could bring out the best in anyone), because she really loved doing it. She coordinated those lessons green. Or when she learned that boys aren't too into girls whose favorite past time is "excavating," especially if you use that word to answer the "what do you like to do" question. She had been blinded by the norms of teenage*ism*, so much that on some days, she'd hide out on 'her farm' to dig herself out from under all the cruel things said to and about her. She hadn't tried to be odd, it just happened. She would aim to be more socially acceptable, since, now she could see! She coordinated those lessons indigo. Or when she learned the VISION that her spirit had always had for herself, that her body was belatedly privy to, as her mind helped the VISION manifest. It came to her after one of her impromptus 'doings' for her parents whereas when they were offering her various incentives, she blurted out, "I actually would like to go on an excavation excursion on the volcanic mountain Mt. Vesuvius off the European continent in the city of Pompeii near Naples." They stopped, stared and stood from where they formerly sat. They paced. They sat again. NOW, she waited. They were in awe, to say the least. "I need to go on this trip," she said, after minutes passed. "Well, what happened to (just) doing it to be be doing it," her mother asked, stunned. "I don't think I was ever *just doing it to be doing it,* she answered, even though I was *just* doing it." "Now, what I want to do with it has *just* evolved, she said." She was seventeen and wanted this trip in place of the senior trip to England. They looked stupefied. She waited some more, because that's what NOW called for. "Where is this all coming from," her father asked interrogatively, as if she was put on or up to it by a teacher. She paused before answering, trying to discern the merit behind the question. Then with unabated conviction, she answered him - them, "I want to be an archeologist and excavate caves of human origin in Africa." She left them to themselves because NOW she understood that she had to. She coordinated those lessons rose pinkish violet.

She waited for a response. Two weeks passed. THEN, they wanted to talk to her. "There's too much to do to get you prepared for that trip," her father said. We don't have the time. "But Dad," she said, "I'm already mostly ready." She showed him her list. There were red X'es on most of the words. Passport. Traveler's Cheques. Contact Host Family. Currency. Language Book. Culture Lessons. Emergency Contact Card. Abroad Travel Health Card. Skype Account on Computer. Travel Money Belt. Audio/Visual Logging Equipment.

My Vision, My Plan, MY NOW

Microscope w/Slides. Protective Eye Gear. Study Boots. Specimen Cases. Helmet. Old Clothes. Workman Gloves. Head Lamp. Knee & Elbow Pads. Of the 20 things on the list, 15 of the items had red X's through them. "No, you're not ready," her father confronted. "Look at all these red X'es of things you haven't done yet. She chuckled. They looked quizzical at each other, him trying to decipher why she was laughing, her, realizing that *he* had forgotten. She didn't say anything. She simply went in towards her room with them in tow. "Look," she said. She pulled out her journals. He skimmed them. They were filled with red X's. "I did all of *those* too," she said. "Wasn't it you who said I just do things differently?" she reminded him. He teared, slightly ashamed for his disbelief in her. "When did you do all this?" her mother asked. "Well," she said coyly, "honestly, since I told you guys, I kind of did something each time I felt like NOW was a moment that I didn't want to loose without being productive towards something I really believed in and wanted for myself." Now, they were smiling while tearing. It wasn't her who wasn't ready. It was them. "So?" she asked. "Of course you can go," her mother said. "You've been PLANNING for this for your whole life.

...

The air was blowing harder, as if to wake her up. She laughed at herself. "I guess I can get into trances now, even without digging." It was time. Her spirit was NOW rejuvenated too. So much time had passed - over two decades since her graduate professors had told her that her insight could land her anywhere. She had done well - very well. "You're still here," came a familiar voice. "Are you okay?" came another familiar voice. They were coming towards her. "You're going to get sand on your clothes," her mother chided playfully. "She's fine," her father chimed. Her mother smiled. Their 'little girl' *was* okay. "Thank You," she said and hugged them warmly, "for allowing me to follow my VISION to *see* myself as I *felt* myself all those years back" she said. "I'm going to get ready. "You already are," her father said as she headed off. "Do you remember when she first said she wanted to be an archeologist," her father reminisced?" "Of course," her mother answered, "I thought she was just excited to let us know that she knew the name of the people who do what she had been doing for so long." "That was almost thirty years ago," her father said. "Yes, just about," her mother said, "but, when you 1) see something for yourself (VISION) and you constantly PLAN for it until it comes, you experience continuous NOW moments in *that* life." "Woah, who's *digging* now," her father said, mischievously. They chuckled and walked on over to the conference.

Doctors Without Borders is honored to introduce you to the lead anthropologist on this seven year excursion excavating the Nile River. Now, this scientist, who's name I am deliberately withholding from you because there is an anecdote attached to her name (her parents looked at each other puzzled) singlehandedly, with her initial research and findings convinced Global Health Organizations to fund this project...indefinitely. Her mission: to dig within various natural elements environments to study the varying effects the elements have on the people who live there. Specifically, she was interested in *discovering* how significantly different (or not) genealogy can be changed with people who's physiological make-up was mostly the same based upon whether the sun greeted those people from the Atlantic Ocean versus the Pacific Ocean. Simply, she asked, do we have a more or less favorable physical disposition based on which body of water we are more connected to plus the sun? As you can imagine, the rest of the science world scrutinized her since there was so many other unfinished projects. Her project was politely declined. In lieu, she accepted a position that was opening in six months to do ethnographic work in Northern Africa. She had time. "I'm going to go Now," she had said. She did. She spent most of her time on the Sahara Desert and the Nile River, living among Nomadic Nilotics.' "By the way, didn't she first begin digging on a beach," the moderator rhetorically asked, momentarily peering at her parents. 'Then she did what she's always done. She dug! She charted. She surveyed. She logged. She hypothesized. She created basic analysis. By six months end, she had had enough data to create a report. That report became the basis for this lecture. Her excavations have discovered pieces of human fossils along various points along the Nile. Upon further research, it was determined that physical features varied slightly to more than slightly based on 'how much sun' a particular country got. The health effects inversely changed as well. He paused. He took off his glasses. He exhaled.

The African people say our names define us. I once asked *this* doctor the origin of her name. She said, "Honestly, I don't know. I never dug for its meaning." Everyone laughed. "Well, I asked her parents about her name's origin, the moderator continued. They told me they met during a study abroad program from their respected universities and the African who introduced them told them that if they had a daughter, to name her Kutam. Kutam loosely translates to 'seeker.' Ladies and Gentleman, please welcome Dr. Kutam Mays. Kutam walked onto the stage and smiled ready to share her New Vision, New Plan, New Now!

NYSHEVA-STARR

Nysheva-Starr is an innovator, writer, designer, speaker, and performing artist. She is the CEO of I-Gaian, Inc, a company primarily aimed at fostering cumulative growth for African Americans. She is the founder, creator, and arranger of Safari Kwenye Nafsi: Journey to Self, the African American Right to Rites of Passage Experience, a comprehensive and progressive series of passages geared towards documenting age set journeys for Black Americans. She has written a series of books which will be published soon, highlighting the principles that make early development successful, especially as it relates to Blacks. As an innovator/designer, she recently patented a garment she made for yoga practitioners.

Follow her on twitter at **@nyshevastarr**. For more information on the passages, send an email to **info@i-gaianinc.com** and/or visit the website at **www.i-gaiainc.com**.

166:

T.A.G. You're It!

Damon Nash

So you want to know how to achieve any and everything you want in life? Ok, then you will need to play a simple game called T.A.G. T.A.G. stands for Thoughts Action and Goals.

I am about to share with you a simple equation that will allow you to get whatever you want. The key to getting whatever you want is to align your Thoughts with your goals. I will share with you how this works in the next couple of pages. But before you read on you need to ask yourself, "Am I ready?" You see with knowledge comes power, and with power comes responsibility. Most people say they want success but secretly are afraid to achieve it.

If you are ready, let's go!!!

Thoughts

For this to work you have to understand how things happen in life. Everything on this earth started with a "Thought." From the clothes you wear, to the car you drive, to the book in your hand. Someone had to think it first. Thoughts are the key and the first step in getting everything that you want.

But not just *having* thoughts, because you have had many thoughts up to this point in your life. But gaining control of your thoughts is the key to the equation. If you can gain better control of your thoughts, then it will take you where ever you would like to go.

So that brings up the big question, "How do I control my thoughts?"

To understand how you control your thoughts you have to understand where your thoughts come from. Your thoughts are the sum of your environment. What you see, hear, and the people you allow in that environment. If you can take control of those three aspects you will gain control of your thoughts. More importantly you can direct your thoughts to you help you do whatever you choose. Let's take a closer look at these three aspects one by one.

With all three aspects you have to understand that you are in control. So when it comes to Sight (seeing) you may not have control of what you see but you do have control of what you Focus on. Try this exercise. Extend your right arm out in front of your face. Now extend your index finger and focus on the index finger. What you should see now is that everything around the index finger is blurry. You can still see it, but it is blurry. Now change your focus, from your index finger to the back ground. You should now notice that your index finger is getting blurry. What you have now experienced is control over focus. When it comes to your thoughts, what will help you gain control is focusing on what you want. Remember you may not have control of what you see but you have control of what you focus on.

The next step in gaining control of your thoughts is hearing vs listening. Again you cannot control what you hear, but you have complete control of what you listen to. Try this the next time you hold a conversation or watch TV. While holding a conversation with someone, switch your focus and listen to all of the noise around you and the conversation. You may hear the A/C or other people talking. You may hear rain outside or a dog barking. The idea behind this is simple… we choose who and what we listen to. Even now as I am writing this, I hear my son playing and laughing at the TV. I also hear the TV along with the refrigerator making ice. But if you can master and truly understand the difference between what you hear versus what you listen to then you are one step closer to gaining control of your own thoughts.

This last part is a very important one: PEOPLE!!!! Again you have complete control on this last step as well. The people you allow in your life have a huge effect on you ultimately reaching your goals. Having the right people in your life can either tear you down or lift you up to heights beyond your wildest dreams. The first two aspects of controlling your thoughts, sight versus focus and hearing versus listening supports what you do with people in your life.

For example: There will be many people who come across your path that you will see, but you have control on who you FOCUS on. You need to focus on a mentor, coach or anyone who can help you to achieve your goal. Also with hearing vs. listening, you will hear a lot of people who will tell you almost anything. But you have control on who you listen to. When it comes to people you, want and need to attach yourself to people that you can learn from. If you are the smartest person in the room, then you are in the wrong room!! Also connect yourself with people who are doing what you want to do, or who have similar interest that will help you.

The key to controlling Thoughts lie in Focusing on and Listening to the right People. By doing this you will create the right environment that will take us to the next step in T.A.G.

Actions

Actions are pretty easy at this point. Without much effort you will find yourself doing things differently once you change and take control of how you think. Once you get around the right people you will have new experiences and will see things differently. These new experiences will bring new activities and opportunities that will take you closer and closer to your goal. The key here is not to procrastinate, and not to be afraid. Many of these actions will be new to you. Whenever you are stepping outside of your comfort zone there is always a touch of fear. Remember with new focus and listening to the right people, you will have new experiences. Here are a few things to remember:

1. Start now
2. Attack this new action with everything you got
3. Remember to learn from each action
4. Failure is part of the process

With actions you also need to realize the power of small wins. Every step you take no matter how small it is towards your goal is important. We love to celebrate the big wins, but it takes the small wins to build confidence. It takes small wins to reach the goals you have set for you. It is increasingly important to embrace small wins when you are doing something that takes you out of your comfort zone.

Goals

The last part is Goals. Remember what we need to do is align our thoughts with our goals. By doing so it will drive actions to achieve whatever goal you have. Now the big question is what are your goals? Goal setting is a powerful process for thinking about your ideal future, and for motivating yourself to turn your vision of this future into reality.

The process of setting goals helps you choose where you want to go in life. By knowing precisely what you want to achieve, you know where you have to concentrate your efforts. You'll also quickly spot the distractions that can, so easily, lead you astray. "Nothing on earth moves unless it is sold that includes your Dreams and your GOALS."

Here are a few examples on goals and how this works.

Goal: Graduate from College

1. Focus on studies.
2. Listen to professors.
3. Network/meet people that are in your major, getting good grades and involved.

Goal: Lose Weight

1. Focus on working out and eating right.
2. Listen to trainer and coaches.
3. Network/meet people who also are looking to lose weight, or work that you can work-out with.

By playing T.A.G (Thoughts Action Goals) you will be able to achieve any goal, and live a happier successful life!!!! T.A.G. You're It!

Damon Nash

Damon is originally from Cleveland OH, where he played High School basketball which earned him a full athletic scholarship to Miles College in Birmingham AL. Damon discovered his passion for motivational speaking while at Miles College and started an on campus group called H.O.A. which stood for Helping Others Achieve. With this organization, Damon and other Miles college students travelled to different High Schools in the area to speak on college and job preparation topics. He graduated from Miles with a degree in Business Administration.

Damon's mission is to influence struggling urban youth to find a path out of the poverty cycle that holds them down. He founded INFLUENCE ENTERTAINMENT INC, a youth empowerment company, where he regularly speaks at schools and churches in the area. To compliment his talks, Damon also created a "hot" t-shirt line called NFLUENCE ME. As one of Monster's "Making It Count" certified speaker he has the opportunity to speak in high schools throughout the southeast and east coast. His mixture of motivational speech and spoken word has been said to not only entertain but really bring the message home.

facebook.com/nfluenceme

Wealth is a Journey

Lonnie Mathews

Let's talk for a few moments about wealth or being wealthy, first let me say that I believe that wealth is a journey rather than a point in time. It's a process, it's a state of mind that takes continued effort to obtain and maintain but most of all wealth is relative.

Yep its relative, not your relative being wealthy and you not being wealthy *(sorry I couldn't resist)*. What I mean is that you don't necessarily have to be a multimillionaire to be considered wealthy. Being wealthy is not based on how much you have but rather what you do with what you have. I am convinced that people with lots of money are not or can't be anymore happier than those of US who don't have lots of money.

I refuse to believe that having MONEY is the basis of my happiness, don't get me wrong I do realize that having money will make life more enjoyable but not happier. I said all of that to say that wealth is relative to your lifestyle needs. If you lead a modest lifestyle, a life where you are personally happy with where you are in life and you somehow manage to live below your means financially then two things will happen.

(1) You will live a much happier life (2) you will eventually build financial wealth over time. Just because someone makes a lot of money doesn't make them wealthy, especially if their expenses are equal to their income or in some cases exceeds their income. If a person looks wealthy and smells wealthy doesn't mean they are. How many times have you seen someone in a fancy car let's say a foreign luxury car, and thought that person must have a lot of money? Did you realize that the number of foreign luxury cars that are leased outnumber the number of cars sold? So is this person wealthy? Anyone with a calculator and common sense can figure out that leasing is the worst way to own or should I say drive an automobile.

If you are not currently wealthy and you would like to become wealthy then you only have to do one thing and that thing is CHANGE! If you are not where you want to be financially, physically, emotionally, spiritually etc… all you have to do is CHANGE, change everything about you, the people you meet, the books you read, and most of all the habits that are currently a part of your everyday routine. If you want to change your financial life you must change the way you are doing things, and the reason you must change is BECAUSE WHAT YOU ARE DOING IS NOT WORKING!

If there is to be any difference in your financial life you cannot be the same person doing the same thing and expecting something different. The first thing you should change is your paradigm of thinking, what I mean is you should think of your personal finances as if you are running a small business. The businesses income is your salary and the business expenses are your current monthly bills and they need to be managed.

Imagine for a moment if you were a CEO of a company and someone in the finance department was handling the business finances the way you are currently handling them would you fire that person?

Maybe you will, maybe you won't, but if the company is not going in the direction that it should you would agree that something needs to be changed. If your company has gotten off track financially you must fire your old-self and hire a new you. Every business that is successful has a net profit each month, which is money left over at the end of each month to invest back into the business. You must examine your financial situation and see if you have a net profit or loss every month. Think of yourself as the CEO and the CFO and you must get this company on the right track financially. Many of the worlds wealthy individuals think of their finances both personally and business in terms of income and expenses and profits.

Do You Have What It Takes to Be Rich?

Being rich or having wealth is a state of mine, in addition to it being a state of mind it's a thought process, and it's a series of habits that keep you pointed in the right direction. The path to wealth is a relative easy one, all you have to do is spend less than you earn and save regularly and that's it. Over time you will build wealth, so why there aren't more wealthy people than there are in the world? The truth is most people lack the willingness to change their current lifestyle and spending habits. Remember building wealth is a way of life; it's like getting into really good physical shape, to stay in shape you have to continue to do the things that got you in shape in the first place.

Most people also lack the discipline to become wealthy, it's not easy to change what you have been doing most of your life. You have to develop a level of "stick-to-it-ness" most people just give up to easily. There are also a lot of misconceptions when it comes to building wealth like "if I were wealthy my problems would go away", "more people would like me if I had money" and "if I were wealthy, I could buy anything that I wanted" Part of what makes wealthy people wealthy is their ability to say "NO". The difference between being wealthy and middle-class is being to afford anything you want but choosing not to anyway. When I was broke I would go the mall and buy anything that I wanted even if it meant that I had to buy it on credit, or I would say things like "When I get some money I'm going to buy..." In other words I really couldn't afford it in the first place, but I bought it anyway.

Now that I have a higher level of understanding about money and I have developed discipline and good habits I could go to the same mall and have the ability to purchase just about anything in there that I wanted but I choose not too instead. That's what makes me wealthy; because of my new attitude I am wealthier in a lot of ways.

Attitude of Abundance

We can change our lives by changing our attitude and with a new attitude comes a new outlook; a new outlook will change your actions. If you believe that you can't or won't ever have wealth then you're right you won't. Building wealth is about believing that you can build wealth and then going out and doing the things that will build wealth. You must have an attitude of abundance and then you will have abundance.

What keeps many of us from doing something new is the fear of failure. Imagine the possibilities you would have in life if you didn't fear failing. One day my wife made the comment that "on any given day most people don't give life their best because they might fail." I think what she was trying to say is that we don't try hard because what happens if we try our best and still fail? How would you react if you tried your best and your best wasn't good enough? So for that reason most of us don't try hard that way we could always say "well I didn't try very hard anyway" I think that most of us don't try hard because we might actually succeed, what happens if we really tried hard to do something and succeed? Then what? You can't just go back to what you were doing; you will have to look for another challenge.

Try This!

Make a short list of three things that you would absolutely do if you knew you would accomplish without failing. Go ahead write down three things that you would do if you knew that there was no way possible for you to fail. Now write a plan to achieve those three things. Now ask yourself what's holding you back?

All too often we get stuck in our comfort zone and that's what keeps us trapped in our current position. It's those comfort zones that keeps us from achieving our goals. I like to say that *"until the pain of your current situation becomes greater than the pain of change, you won't change"* I want to challenge you to get out of your comfort zone, do something different, do something that you always wanted to do, go ahead I dare you to try. Don't be afraid to make a mistake don't be afraid of failure. *"To succeed is to fail and to fail is to succeed"* Making mistakes is the opportunity to learn, mistakes teach you what not to do the next time you try, that is if you try a next time. One of the biggest reasons people aren't wealthy is because they never tried. If you find yourself off course because of a mistake just retrace your steps find the mistake make the necessary corrections and keep moving forward. Remember wealth is a journey not a destination. You must make the decision to seek wealth and if you do then you will find it, but you have to make the first step on a life journey.

Choices

With every dollar that comes into our lives we have a choice. We have the choice on how the dollars that we have earned today will shape our lives tomorrow. What we do with the dollars that we earn will determine if we will be rich, poor or middle class in the future. In the book *"The millionaire Next Door"* authors Dr. Thomas Stanley and Dr. William Danko discovered some amazing facts about individuals who started with little or no wealth and over time accumulated a net worth of more than one million dollars. The two things that all of these individuals had in common no matter what their backgrounds were or how they accumulated their wealth was.

Number one they lived well below their means, and were very frugal with their money. The study showed that the average self-made millionaire drove a two to three year old car. The second thing that individuals who became millionaires did the most to become wealthy was they spent their time and resources on ways to build wealth. In other words these individuals didn't waste a lot of their time purchasing and displaying high status items. This means that they didn't purchase status items like expensive luxury cars and over the top homes.

The first choice that you must make if you ever want to become wealthy is to control your spending. I realized that may sound easy but trust me it is a very difficult thing to accomplish. Controlling and ultimately reducing your current spending means that you must control the desire to consume. Let's face it no one ever sets out to over spend; they just don't have a plan not to overspend. Controlling the desire to consume is a lot of work, especially when you consider that every minute of the day we are bombarded with advertisements from companies jockeying for your hard earned dollars. When you think about it there are really only three things that you can do with the money that you earn. (1) You could spend it (2) You could save or invest it and (3) You could give it away. No matter what action you take with money it will fall into one of these three areas. The trick to being financially wealthy is to find a healthy balance among the three.

For most people we focus all of our time on the spending part and not enough on the saving and giving parts. If you ever want to get ahead financially you must learn to control your spending. Unfortunately, just like Parkinson's Law states our everyday expenses tend to rise to meet our income. It's like as soon as you get a raise or some additional income you find ways for it to become consumed. Make today the day you take a stance against over spending, today is the day you draw a line in the sand, and today is the day you say no more. Once you have the attitude that I want to change here's what you do. Take a serious look at your current spending and decide some areas that you could cut. At first glance you my say "hey there is nothing to cut; I NEED to spend money on the things that I am spending them on now". Really do you absolutely need all those cable channels? Do you really need that gym membership because you go to the gym every day right?

I think you get the point. There are thousands of ways to cut your spending, and there are plenty of books and articles out there for you to read and come up with ways to reduce your spending. The trick is you really have to want to reduce your spending and change your lifestyle to get where you want to be financially. The biggest reason that you don't have more money saved; the biggest reason that you aren't where you want to be financially is YOU!

"To conquer life we must first conquer ourselves"

I like this quote because it sums up most people's financial problems in a very short and to the point statement. This statement simply says that for your financial life to get where you want it to be you must find a way to control your spending which means that you must find a way to control you. I could go on and on about how to control your spending and finding ways to cut back but I won't, I will leave that up to you to decide when and where you will control your spending and change your life.

LONNIE MATHEWS

Lonnie Mathews is a motivational financial speaker who empowers audiences with tools and strategies to make immediate and long-term shifts in their lives. Lonnie has worked as a financial advisor and is the author two books on personal finance. His latest title *Spend Everything – an inspirational guide to money management* is available where books are sold. Lonnie now travels the country delivering his powerful and life changing messages on personal finance. Lonnie is a dynamic and engaging speaker who gets audiences excited about taking charge of their financial futures.

Lonnie@lonniemathews.com / www.lonniemathews.com

My Vision, My Plan, MY NOW

Building a Winning Personal Brand in a Digital World

Michael Tucker

I remember sitting in the lunch room on my first day of High School. As I looked around the cafeteria, I noticed that people seemed to separate themselves into groups. The first group I noticed was "the popular group." This group was filled with kids that were the epitome of cool. They wore the latest brands, knew the newest music and always seemed to know the juiciest school gossip. Then there was the Goth group, I never really figured this group out but from what I could tell, they all seemed to share a love for wearing black and discussing being misunderstood by society. The jocks and nerds also had their own tables, group norms and values.

After realizing that I was now in the middle of a world where everyone seemed to self-identify with a group, I soon became confronted with the fact that I was sitting alone. The longer I sat, the louder the thoughts of my mind became. I was faced with a question I had never considered before. How would I define myself over the next four years? Would I become a part of an existing group or would I create my own path? How would others define me? How would I define myself?

My Vision, My Plan, MY NOW

What I did not realize was at that very moment, I was asking the type of questions that would eventually lead me to become a personal brand that would be forever seared in the subconscious minds of my high school friends, peers and teachers. My choice would not only decide where I might end up sitting in the cafeteria, It would also determine where I might sit in class, the type of grades I could expect to receive, and how people would interact with me. Additionally, my choice would shape my experience of the world and the reputation I would eventually build for myself.

None of the groups sitting at the tables previously mentioned stood out to me. My clothes were clean but as the son of an auto mechanic and stay-at-home mom with four children, I was far from fashionable. I never fully understood the Goth group. I enjoyed playing sports and played regularly. However, I was not a jock and even though I was usually an honor roll student I could never pass for a nerd.

After a few weeks passed I became aware of another group that interested me almost instantly. It was the students in the Army JROTC program. There were nearly 500 students in this program at my high school. Amidst the 5 companies that made up our JROTC battalion, there were two very elite teams; the rifle team and the drill team. Members of these teams didn't wear the standard issue military shoes or the envelope-looking service cap the other cadets wore. Instead, they wore neatly polished boots and burgundy or black berets. They had a chest full of ribbons, and metals, and were respected by other cadets as well as the teachers and faculty. The rifle team mastered shooting .22 caliber rifles and won marksmanship competitions up and down the east coast.

The drill team was comprised of 30 of the sharpest cadets in the battalion. They were experts in performing all of the Army's basic drill and ceremony practices. They also synchronized, the spinning, tossing and catching of 10 pound, Springfield, M1903 rifles in close proximity of other each other. Drill team members were the best dressed of the two teams and their craft was impressive, dangerous, and very alluring. Like the rifle team, the Lower Richland High drill team had taken first place in numerous competitions on the east coast and was known as a fierce competitor by high schools throughout South Carolina.

After a month of physically exhausting tryouts that consisted of ungodly amounts of push up, standing perfectly still at attention for hours and performing marching, facing and rifle movements until I could no longer feel my body, I would go on to earn my place as a member of the drill team. In my senior year I would become 2nd in command of the battalion and one of two Co-Captains for the drill team. Additionally, I would earn two letters for my letterman jacket and build a reputation for myself as an excellent student and leader among my peers. This would eventually translate in to being accepted to the University of South Carolina, the Opportunity Scholars Program, a merit-based federal program designed to provide financial and academic support to low-income students. I would also go on to earn two scholarships.

Fast forward through my undergraduate studies, four years of leading troops as a commissioned Air Force Officer, two years of a Master's degree program and six years as an entrepreneur, international speaker and marketing professional and you end up with the story you now read. After all of the previously mentioned experiences it was only about four years ago after I entered the marketing profession that I realized I had been building a personal brand my entire life.

Like most people I was completely unconscious of what I was creating. Fortunately, I had great mentors and made several good choices along the way. Sadly, this was not the case for a number of my friends. The purpose of this chapter is to help you consciously create your personal brand and ultimately your life.

What is a personal brand?

Simply put, a personal brand is what people come to know and expect from you on a tangible and intangible or emotional level; It's your reputation and how it makes others feel. Take a moment to think of someone you admire. How do you feel when you think about this person? What are the first images and words that come to mind when you hear their name? What is their expertise? Would this be the first person you called if you needed help in that area? Is the person you're thinking of confident, a great leader, communicator, technologist, problem solver, innovator, etc? Do they motivate and inspire you to give your best effort? These are all possible characteristic of a compelling personal brand.

Personal branding is important because society values consistency, predictability, and requires clear distinctions in order to sort through a world cluttered with choices. Furthermore, taking ownership of your brand leaves less room for interpretation about who you are and how you'd like to be known. Your actions and reputation will precede you. Do you have friends or relatives that are always searching for a "hook up," "lucky break" or "the right connection" to get what they desire in life?

This type of thinking is lottery-based and a by-product of self-doubt. Self-doubt can be overcome by building confidence. Confidence is created by setting and achieving several small but meaningful goals. Choosing courage and intentionally developing a personal brand also helps one to build self-belief. When you build a reputable personal brand, friends, family, coworkers, and the world, will know exactly what you stand for and what gifts you have to bear. They will share your worth with others and new opportunities will seek you out.

What's *your* personal brand?

It's never too early or too late to start thinking about building a personal brand. Oprah Winfrey, Justin Bieber, General Colin Powell, and Barbara Walters are all personal brands. Each of them represents different values and occupies the number one position in the minds of millions for their category of business or expertise. Like well-known consumer brands (McDonalds, Coca Cola, Kleenex), these individuals all started with a dream and a plan. What is your dream? Do you have a personal branding plan to support it?

Stop reading for a moment and ponder this question. How will you package and communicate your values to the world through action? Make a list of these values as well as a list of interest, passions and talents. How can you use these values and interest to position yourself in the minds of others as unique and valuable? Take a few minutes to think about your life mission; first as a human and then as a professional? Are the two in alignment with each other? Why or why not? Flash forward into the future. Based on your current course of action how will you realize these values and interest throughout life? How will you help others realize their values? If you were listening from beyond death would you be pleased with what you hear? Has your time in this world been equivalent to the splash of a pebble or that of a kid doing cannon balls at a neighborhood pool party?

My life mission is to "Explore the world, do lasting good and leave a legacy of love and abundance." Professionally, I have chosen to become a recognized leader in social media and mobile marketing and a social entrepreneur (one that uses business principles to solve social problems). My personal mission statement is my north star. It guides me through life and ultimately shapes and defines my values. What is your personal mission statement? Your professional brand should align with this mission statement and help others know when to call on you for support.

NOTE: When people contact you for your expertise, they generally don't expect to receive your help for free. When they show up, don't be afraid to bill them. This actually strengthens your position in their mind as the expert they are looking for. It also allows them to eliminate shame associated with receiving something for nothing. Allow others to share their abundance with you.

Being paid for sharing unique expertise is known as consulting if one remains independent and takes on multiple clients or key employment if he/she chooses to work exclusively for a company. Consulting or key employment positions are only gained by someone with real or perceived value. These positions are usually unadvertised and they tend to pay exceptionally well. To obtain a solid consulting or key employment position you must be recommended to someone of power with a need by another of influence. What brand have you created for yourself among people of influence in your city or industry? Are they aware of your work, your values, and what inspires you? If not what is your plan to help them become aware?

The idea that one can merely advertise themselves by handing out resumes and/or submitting job applications to strangers in order to gain employment is lazy thinking. This alone will not work in today's global and highly competitive economy.

Creating your brand

Creating a personal brand allows you to focus your energy and obtain the highest value for your efforts. It also assists others in quickly finding the support they need as they pursue their dreams and goals.

NOTE: Your brand is about you but its function is not for your sake alone. It serves as a guide to assist others in seeking you out as the solution for their unique problems. The success of your personal brand is measured by how well people receive your message and engage with you as a result of it.

After you have identified your personal mission and expertise or the industry you'd like to be associated with, make an effort to study and learn all you can about this interest or industry. If you are unclear about what this interest is, explore your past and participate in different activities until you can identify the interest that captures your mind and inspires your heart. When you become aware of the interest seek to master it.

I once heard it said that one can become an expert on almost any matter, industry, or industry niche by following a few simple steps;

First, read the top five books about the topic then, complete the top four online courses, attend the top three conferences and regularly converse with as many experts in that industry as possible. One can also take on a project(s) that will allow learning through experience. After you have completed these steps you should begin to think of yourself as an expert on the topic. No other permission is required unless your subject matter resides in the domain of licensed professionals. If you are seeking to gain expertise in an area that requires mandated training or licensure please add this to the steps mentioned above. Practicing medicine, law or any other profession that requires licensure illegally can bring about consequences that are destructive to your personal brand.

If you are currently pursuing a career that requires licensure, the aforementioned method can aid you in learning more about your profession and/or mastering a specific niche within it. A perfect example would be Attorney John Pestle. John is a family friend who practices law at Varnum Law Firm. Unlike his colleagues, instead of focusing on traditionally competitive areas of business law (Tax, intellectual property rights, or investment law) He has made a name for himself by becoming a legal expert in cell phone tower leasing and zoning law. At this time he is one of less than a hundred American attorneys that specialize in this subject matter. You can visit John's blog at Varnumlaw.com/blogs/cell-phone-tower/. Mastering and strategically promoting niche expertise within an industry can mean the difference between making a living and making a fortune. As the saying goes, "Get rich in a niche."

Living your Brand

Live your brand by making a contribution and consistently sharing what you are learning with others. You can accomplish this in a number of ways offline and online. Offline, you can attend national and international conferences and social events, promote key industry interest and related causes, author white papers, articles, reports, chapters of books, e-books, or books, host informational presentations or training classes, and volunteer to support a project, industry organization or its leaders.

Sharing your brand online can be done by posting content developed for offline consumption along with other engaging, educational, or entertaining, information to Facebook, Twitter, Google Plus and/or your YouTube account regularly. It is also important to thoroughly complete your LinkedIn profile, get recommendations, join interest-related groups, and answer questions people are asking about your area of interest. Recommend others on LinkedIn, comment regularly on blogs and regularly write your own. Doing so will ensure your name and content show up in online searches when others are looking for information about your topic of interest.

You can call your blog "YourName.com." Get a local web designer to set up a WordPress blog on a web host like Hostgator or Godaddy. Make sure you also buy a domain name and create a header graphic that consist of a professional headshot and text communicating your expertise. Hosting a blog should cost roughly $10-$15 per month. You and your web designer should choose the best theme, colors and layout to represent your brand. It is always a good idea to borrow ideas from other industry related blogs you enjoy reading.

Setting up a simple blog should cost less than a few hundred dollars. However, the more customized the blog, the more you can expect to pay. If you are tech savvy and can follow directions in a YouTube video you should be able set up a simple blog for the price of the hosting and domain name only. Stay away from free or unhosted blogs as it is not uncommon for free or unhosted blog providers to become the legal owner of the content you produce.

Additionally, free blogging platforms generally limit the user's ability to fully customize his/her blog by restricting the use of various plugins and third party software like email list building tools. To see an example of a personally branded blog, you can visit my blog; MrMichaelTucker.com.

Final Thoughts

Creating a personal brand on and offline is not just a good idea. It is critical for anyone that seeks to compete and stand out as a professional in the 21st century. Developing a brand demonstrates your clarity of focus and proves that you are proactively guiding your life instead of passively waiting for success to one day knock on your door. It also shows your willingness to make a contribution to an area of interest or industry and the stakeholders that support it.

Build your brand with intention, passion and strategy while, while creating mutually beneficial relationships, that support the brands and causes of others. This simple yet thoughtful act will introduce you to successes beyond anything you could have ever imagined.

MICHAEL TUCKER

Michael Tucker is an international speaker, trainer and consultant as well as the founder and CEO of Social Mobile Buzz, a marketing and communications company specializing in turning inspiring professionals and companies into champion brands through the use of social media and mobile marketing. Social Mobile Buzz represents small, mid-sized and large clients in the corporate, non-profit, and government sectors. Michael earned his bachelor's degree in Retail Management from the University of South Carolina and a master's in Human Relations from the University of Oklahoma. He currently lives in Tucson with his wife Ellen.

MrMichaelTucker.com
Twitter @mrmichaeltucker
michael@socialmobilebuzz.com

My Vision, My Plan, MY NOW

Is There a Book in You?
Andrea Foy

The best way to make your dreams come true is to wake up! - Paul Valery

Just Do It!

Is there a book in you? How about a marathon, climbing Mt. Kilimanjaro? Becoming a chef? What is on your bucket list? When you do dream, what do you see? What did you want to be when you were a kid? What do you want to be known for when you leave this world?

My dream was a book. For as long as I can remember, I have wanted to be an author; to see my name on a book. It was my dream. I loved to write as a child and a teenager, I had a vivid and active imagination and could make up stories easily. I loved to entertain people.

It wasn't until 5th grade that I realized I actually had an aptitude for writing. My teacher sent me home with a writing certificate for my parents and told them to 'Keep her writing.' A High school, Creative Writing English teacher tried to get me to enter a Community College writing contest in the teen fiction genre based on my writing for the class–but of course I was a surly teenager and way too cool for that!

By the time I went to college, I realized that this writing thing might work out because writing was effortless for me. I majored in Communications and wanted to become a news anchor but life got in the way and I ended up not writing at all for years after college. Ironically after travelling the world as a flight attendant, living in Atlanta and Minneapolis, I ended up back home and met a local Christian author, Vanessa Miller, by coincidence while out shopping with my aunt. My aunt told Vanessa that I *was* a writer and she autographed her self-published book, **'Just do it, write, write, write.'** I went home that very night and outlined a fiction book. My writer's block completely vanished and I wrote like a wild woman for months. I sent Vanessa an email, thanking her for the inspiration and the next year in 2004, she sent me an invitation to a writer's conference, given by her and Valerie Coleman. There I learned the craft of writing from Vanessa and the business of selling a book from Valerie. I went to these conferences for 5 years and in 2010, Valerie published, **Hire Power: How to Find, Get, And Keep a Job!** There it was! My name! Some people have always wanted to see their name in lights. This is good enough for me.

Now obviously I am not famous and no Oprah never called (I am still sitting by the phone though, just in case) but being a published author still is one of my proudest moments. Not even completing grad school matched the feeling of accomplishment that publishing this book has done for me.

Now back to you

Have you thought about it? What is it that when you are all alone and quiet, whispers at your soul? Maybe it wakes you up at night. Certainly when you see someone else achieve it, you feel it in your gut.

You wonder why they were so lucky. What do they have that you don't have? So what is holding **you** back?

Step Out On Faith

One of my friends has a goal to be a professional speaker and even buy his own airplane to fly to his presentations all over the world. Now that's an attainable goal, and to do it he gives about 150 speeches a year to whatever audience he can find, scouts, schools, nursing homes, Toastmasters, Rotary, Chamber of Commerce, etc, the list goes on. He still has his day job but it hasn't hindered his dream.

After I wrote *Hire Power*, people kept asking me to give presentations on my book which totally contradicted my idea of writing the book in the first place. I thought to myself, "If I wanted to give presentations, then I would have just given them." But then again maybe it is all part of God's plan. Maybe I was meant to talk to people, not as a journalist or reporter or news anchor but as a speaker and a writer. One thing is for sure. When you are an author, people do see you in a different light. You are considered an expert. I have had many contacts and opportunities open up for me because people have seen or read my book. It is amazing and a blessing!

For those of you that do want to write a book, here are some tips to start with. You can contact me at info@andreafoy.com.

Tips

1. **Ghostwriter** – If the thought of writing out every word and editing and revising nauseates you but you still feel you have

something to say, hire a ghostwriter. These are people who love to write and will partner with you to write a book. Caveat emptor - Let the buyer beware, do your due diligence and research and I am confident you will find a good match. Get samples from them and references. Ask for referrals. Make sure they have a website, bio, etc. Look for professionals only. If you two cannot agree on tone, voice, etc. Get another person and start over. You want your book to be your book, not the ghostwriter's vision of your book.

2. **Editing** – This is extremely important. One of the reasons that spurred me to actually write my own book was a self-published writer who talked me into buying his book. It looked good on the outside and was even a pretty good read but it had so many typos and pure misspellings in it, I couldn't even finish it. I wondered how and why he would try and sell something that had errors! Now I know. You need professional editing from the same sources I suggested for a ghostwriter. Do not use a relative or friend that was good in English in school. Professional is the only way to go.

3. **Dragon Naturally** - This is software I use to dictate to the computer. It takes some getting used to at first, but as soon as you learn each other, it becomes easy. It saves on writer's cramp and carpel tunnel syndrome as well and it is super fast way to write. There are other software products out there, but this is the only one I have tried and I like it.

4. **Mindmapping-** In my book *Hire Power*, I discuss mindmapping as a tool to help people decide what they want to do in life. The same applies to writing a book: The first thing you want to do when writing a book is WRITE IT DOWN! You have no idea how many people have told me that they have a book in their head, they just didn't have time to write it down yet! That gets you no money, fame, recognition and satisfaction. People need to be able to read something on an electronic device or in paper form. Take time to decide what you want to write about.

Mind mapping is a great exercise to help organize chapters and points you want to make. The process starts with a broad theme and then incorporates brainstorming to narrow the focus. Use a sheet of paper or poster board and colored pencils to write what you like or want. For example, if you want to write about jobs that work with animals, take a sheet of paper and write ANIMALS in the center of the paper and then circle it. From the circle draw several lines so that appears to be a sun with rays. The brainstorming component considers different jobs that deal with animals. Write each profession-veterinarian, pet store owner, rescue shelter, as well as just, dog trainer, groomer, etc.-on a different sunray. The next phase of brainstorming looks at each profession in more detail. Consider what the job entails and what it takes to acquire the job. Let's start with veterinarian. Draw several lines under the veterinarian sunray. Words like COLLEGE, INCOME, SICK PETS, SURGERY, EMPLOYEES, etc. will be placed on those lines. Repeat the process for each profession until you have developed a, good list of information. From there, develop the chapters and do the mindmap again. You can almost outline a whole book on one piece of paper once you get the hang of it. There is even software that allows you to mindmap on a computer, but to me that takes away from the creative process. I literally like to use a piece of white paper and colored pencils and draw a picture. I used it for ***Hire Power*** and ***In the Still of the Night: Personal Safety for Women.***

> 5. **What do you love/What do you know about?** ***Hire Power*** came about because I was interviewing for a second job to help pay off my bills when I wanted to buy my home. I went into the HR office of a large retailer to get a holiday job and saw a young adult sitting in the office. She had shorts and tennis shoes on and was slumped over the table. I thought she was waiting for someone who was interviewing, but the *store manager* came out and announced her name and looked at me because I was dressed like I was ready for an interview. She got up, did not make eye contact, nor shake his hand but went into the office behind him. I knew she was not getting the job. I had had no plans to write a book about helping people get a job, I was not an HR expert, but I kept talking to this girl in my head and eventually my head began to hurt and it had to come out. My mother said to me, "You wanted to write a book, there it is!" My point is here that I didn't consider myself an expert but after using the girl as my muse, I have become an expert. ***Hire Power*** was not my choice, it was an obsession. And it is helping a lot of people.

Dan Poynter, the father of self-publishing, became the expert in the same way. He wanted to read a book on hang-gliding but at that time (1973) he couldn't find any, so he wrote his own. Traditional publishers would not publish it, so he printed and published it himself. In 1979, he wrote *The Self Publishing Manual* and the craft was born. He is beyond rich and famous today and has taught his craft to many. He even awarded *Hire Power,* the 2010 Career, non-fiction Global eBook of the year! Now that's an endorsement and an honor!

6. **Self-Publishing** - Self publishing is hard and not for everybody. I was lucky that I found a person like Valerie Coleman (Queen V Publishing) who loved to and wanted to do the details things like, getting a book cover designed, doing the back cover, letting me own the ISBN, editing the book and getting it printed for a reasonable price. I contracted with her to self-publish my own book.

Please know there are some really bad publishers out there. Self-Publishing is a huge business these days. There are people out there who are taking advantage of the trend. They take most of your earnings, charge you too much for your own book, I could go on for days. Research these companies as well. More and more people are trying websites like elance.com and fiverr.com for editing and cover design. I have yet to try these so I can't offer advice.

7. **Traditional Publishing** - It is on the decline but not dead. Back in the day, publishers, mostly in New York would receive 100's of manuscripts from writers. They had the liberty to reject anyone they wanted and many did. Can you believe JK Rowling (Harry Potter) was rejected dozens of times before someone just decided to read her manuscript? Then you get people like the guy who wrote a book full of lies and even got on Oprah to sell millions of copies before he was discovered. He was already rich by then.

Also, say you are accepted, 1- you are subject to the publisher significantly changing your book, (they own it at that point) and 2- the process can take up to two years based on the Publishing Houses' schedule. Who wants to wait around for that when others are literally getting books out in weeks? The point I am trying to make here is you can try a traditional route to publishing a book but the new trend is to do it yourself. Let the powers that be (i.e. the public) decide whether or not it is good, not one person in an office in New York. If the book is good, they will buy it, if it is not, you will learn a great lesson. It will cost you the same amount to self-publish that it would a really nice vacation overseas. I am quite sure you will enjoy the experience just the same!

8. **Marketing** – This by far is the hardest part of being an author. Most people, including me, think that just writing the book and using word of mouth will sell it. Nope, you have to work harder really to sell the book than you do to write it. But, again, people are doing it every day. Even if you use a traditional publisher, they do not market the book for you. Agents and PR people can get costly as well. Right now while you are reading this book, someone else is writing, publishing and selling theirs. (Like me!) And having fun doing it too! The process no matter how hard is extremely fun and satisfying at the end of the day.

Pinky Bunny!

Kristina Cardoza – Early in 2012, I had the pleasure of meeting a 10-year-old author. Her mother is completely supportive of her and I am sure she will be famous one day. Her book is called ***Pink Bunny's First***

Day of School. I feel a connection to her because I wonder what would have happened if I was able to publish my first book at 10.

But then again I know everything happens for a reason and my season seems to be now. Besides it probably wasn't even possible back in the day for kids to publish anything.

9. **Anthologies, et al** The concept for *My Now* is a popular one; get many authors together and let them contribute a chapter. With this concept authors do not have to write 60,000-70,000 words themselves and they can still become a published author! It is great for first-time authors or people that do not have enough material to write a whole book yet. This is my second contribution to this concept. *Single and Loving it: A Handbook for the African American Woman's Guide* had 15 contributors. I have 4 more collaborations due out in 2013, not counting the fiction and e-books I plan to write.

10. **Last but not least, EBooks.** Before you sign a contract to publish physical books, give eBooks a try. You'll save a lot of money. Kindle publishing (KDP Select) and Create Space are good vehicles to try first. KDP is strictly electronic and CS offers an option for the customer to print-on-demand. This way if your book needs work, you can edit it and change it, it is not permanent. You can update and revise your books at a whim. Most of my new books will be electronic, with the option to print from Create Space.

Conclusion:

I hope I haven't discouraged you with all of the work involved in producing a book. <u>Nothing in life that is worth it is easy</u>. Books leave a legacy forever; they should be treated with care and respect.

There are about 50,000 published every year so they must be worth the blood, sweat and tears.

We all have a book in our heads. Hire a ghostwriter, get some software, find some great professionals and get it done! THERE IS A BOOK IN YOU!

In 2013, I plan to revise *Hire Power* and start career coaching. That is **MY VISION, MY PLAN, MY NOW**, what is yours?

The Man in the Arena

"It is not the critic who counts; not the man who points out how the strong man stumbles, or where the doer of deeds could have done them better. The credit belongs to the man who is actually in the arena, whose face is marred by dust and sweat and blood; who strives valiantly; who errs, who comes short again and again, because there is no effort without error and shortcoming; but who does actually strive to do the deeds; who knows great enthusiasms, the great devotions; who spends himself in a worthy cause; who at the best knows in the end the triumph of high achievement, and who at the worst, if he fails, at least fails while daring greatly, so that his place shall never be with those cold and timid souls who neither know victory nor defeat."

~Theodore Roosevelt, Paris, France 1910 (Excerpt from a speech)

ANDREA FOY

Andrea Foy is an award-winning international author, speaker, consultant and coach. She conducts workshops and seminars on topics such as: Women's Issues, Business Skills, Diversity, Image Consulting, Personal Success Strategic Plan and the Hire Power Series. Andrea is a Certified Professional Coach, a Certified Diversity Training Consultant and a Certified Facilitator with Moovin4ward Presentations. She is also an Independent John Maxwell Leadership Coach.

You can reach Andrea at **info@andreafoy.com** or visit her website at **www.andreafoy.com**.

My Vision, My Plan, MY NOW

My Vision, My Plan, MY NOW

Learn More about Moovin4ward Presentations LLC

Programs by Moovin4ward Presentations

- Journey to Success: Personal Success Strategic Plan
- Attitudes of Empowerment
- Moovin4ward 2 College
- Career & Leadership Success

Books by Moovin4ward Publishing

- Mapping Your Journey to Success: Six Strategies for Personal Success

    By Sharon A. Myers & Mark W. Wiggins

- Slumber Party, A story of four girls who pledge to survive high school and life... but didn't.

    By Sharon A. Myers

To bring a certified Moovin4ward speaker to present a program or to purchase any Moovin4ward books and products, visit **www.Moovin4ward.com** or **www.Journey2SuccessPSSP.com**.

www.ingramcontent.com/pod-product-compliance
Lightning Source LLC
Chambersburg PA
CBHW060519100426
42743CB00009B/1374